The Theory of Rules

The Theory of Rules

KARL N. LLEWELLYN

Edited and with an Introduction by
FREDERICK SCHAUER

The University of Chicago Press
Chicago and London

Karl N. Llewellyn (1893–1962) was a major figure in American legal thought and one of the pioneers of American Legal Realism. He taught at Columbia University and the University of Chicago and was the author of such classic works as *The Bramble Bush: On Our Law and Its Study* and *The Common Law Tradition: Deciding Appeals*.

Frederick Schauer is the David and Mary Harrison Distinguished Professor of Law at the University of Virginia. He is the author of *Playing by the Rules: A Philosophical Examination of Rule-Based Decision-Making in Law and in Life* (1991) and *Thinking Like a Lawyer: A New Introduction to Legal Reasoning* (2009).

The University of Chicago Press, Chicago 60637
The University of Chicago Press, Ltd., London

Printed in the United States of America

20 19 18 17 16 15 14 13 12 11   1 2 3 4 5

ISBN-13: 978-0-226-48795-3 (cloth)
ISBN-10: 0-226-48795-4 (cloth)

Library of Congress Cataloging-in-Publication Data

Llewellyn, Karl N. (Karl Nickerson), 1893–1962.
The theory of rules / Karl N. Llewellyn ; edited and with an introduction by Frederick Schauer.
p. cm.
Includes bibliographical references and index.
ISBN-13: 978-0-226-48795-3 (cloth : alk. paper)
ISBN-10: 0-226-48795-4 (cloth : alk. paper) 1. Law—Decision making—Philosophy. 2. Law—Methodology. 3. Decision making—Philosophy. I. Schauer, Frederick F. II. Title.
K230.L485A37 2011
340'.11—dc22

2010025879

♾ The paper used in this publication meets the minimum requirements of the American National Standard for Information Sciences—Permanence of Paper for Printed Library Materials, ANSI Z39.48-1992.

CONTENTS

EDITOR'S INTRODUCTION

The perfect turn of phrase brings costs as well as benefits. The ability to create a memorable line is a valuable talent, but one that can increase the risk that the creator will be remembered for the wrong thing precisely because a vivid wording sticks so firmly in the mind and in history.

So it is with Karl Llewellyn, and with his description of legal rules in *The Bramble Bush* as "pretty playthings."[1] This phrase, in conjunction with Llewellyn's occasional Holmesian focus on law as the prediction of judicial decisions, led H.L.A. Hart to treat Llewellyn as an exemplary "rule skeptic."[2] And numerous others before and since have taken the contemptuousness of the "pretty playthings" language as representing Llewellyn's beliefs in particular and those of the Legal Realists in general about the place of rules in legal decision making.[3]

The view that Llewellyn viewed legal rules as no more than pretty playthings does not even survive a full reading of *The Bramble Bush*, let alone the entire corpus of Llewellyn's work.[4] In fact, when almost thirty years later he

1. "[R]ules . . . are important so far as they help you see or predict what judges will do or so far as they help you get judges to do something. That is their importance. That is all their importance, except as pretty playthings." K.N. Llewellyn, *The Bramble Bush: On Our Law and Its Study* 5 (Columbia 1930).

2. H.L.A. Hart, *The Concept of Law* 135 (Penelope A. Bulloch and Joseph Raz, eds, 2d ed, Oxford/Clarendon 1994).

3. See, for example, George P. Fletcher, *Comparative Law as a Subversive Discipline*, 46 Am J Comp L 683, 687 (1998); Susan Haack, *On Legal Pragmatism: Where Does "The Path of the Law" Lead Us?*, 50 Am J Juris 71, 85 (2005); Heidi Margaret Hurd, Note, *Relativistic Jurisprudence: Skepticism Founded on Confusion*, 61 S Cal L Rev 1417, 1438 (1988); William Simon, *The Ideology of Advocacy: Procedural Justice and Professional Ethics*, 1978 Wis L Rev 29, 39–42.

4. In the 1951 second edition of *The Bramble Bush*, Llewellyn expressed regret that his earlier "unhappy words" had sown so much confusion and misunderstanding. Karl N. Llewellyn, *The Bramble Bush: On Our Law and Its Study* 9 (Oceana, 2d ed 1951). Interestingly, Hart notes

published *The Common Law Tradition: Deciding Appeals*,[5] Llewellyn's opinions about the effect and importance of legal rules had a surprisingly conventional and non-skeptical cast. Nevertheless, Llewellyn's catchy dismissal of rules as "pretty playthings" has helped to frame both him and Legal Realism, and has fostered generations of inaccurate caricatures about the Realist view of legal rules, caricatures that have hindered our understanding not only of Llewellyn and Realism, but also of rules in general and their role in legal decision making.

Believing that his views about legal rules were being widely mischaracterized, Llewellyn commenced work in 1938 on a book he tentatively entitled *The Theory of Rules*. He labored steadily on the manuscript over the ensuing two years, but then turned to other things, including writing about the law of sales and about legal education, as well as conducting the research on legal anthropology that would culminate in *The Cheyenne Way*.[6] Llewellyn may have remained too busy with other projects ever to have returned to this almost-completed book on rules, or perhaps he (mistakenly) believed that everything he had to say about rules would find its way into *The Common Law Tradition*[7] or into his *Law in Our Society* teaching materials,[8] but for whatever reason the manuscript of *The Theory of Rules* remained uncompleted at Llewellyn's death in 1962, and has languished among his papers at the University of Chicago ever since. When William Twining catalogued those papers in 1964–65,[9] he included in the published catalog a chapter from *The Theory of Rules*,[10] but other than that the book manuscript has never seen the light of day.

Llewellyn's partial retreat in H.L.A. Hart, *Positivism and the Separation of Law and Morals*, 71 Harv L Rev 593, 615 n.40 (1958), but for some unexplained reason chose to ignore it three years later when discussing Legal Realism in Chapter VII of *The Concept of Law*. And in a 1942 correspondence with Lon Fuller, Llewellyn, who tended to be prickly about misunderstanding of his own work in particular or that of the Realists in general (see Karl N. Llewellyn, *Some Realism about Realism*, 44 Harv L Rev 1222 (1931)), lamented that few recognized that "[e]ven Bramble Bush p. 3 carried its own correction in Ch. V."

5. Karl N. Llewellyn, *The Common Law Tradition: Deciding Appeals* (Little Brown 1960).

6. Karl Llewellyn and E. Adamson Hoebel, *The Cheyenne Way* (Oklahoma 1941).

7. *The Common Law Tradition*. On the background of this book, see William Twining, *Karl Llewellyn and the Realist Movement* 203–5 (Weidenfeld and Nicolson 1973, reprinted with Postscript, 1985).

8. This important but still unpublished work, as good or better a window into the later Llewellyn as *The Common Law Tradition*, is described in detail in Twining, cited in note 7, at 170–202.

9. William Twining. *The Karl Llewellyn Papers* (Chicago 1968).

10. Id at 81–96. A brief description of the book manuscript also appears in Twining, *Karl Llewellyn and the Realist Movement*, cited in note 7, at 488–93, as part of Twining's summary of Llewellyn's views about legal rules.

The Theory of Rules is important for three reasons. First, it helps frame the development of Llewellyn's own thought, and thus contributes to the intellectual history of one of the major figures in American legal thought. Second, it provides the most sophisticated analysis in existence of the Legal Realist view about rules. *The Common Law Tradition* is a mature, sane, and balanced work, but perhaps so much so that the bite of the characteristic—or at least stronger even if not characteristic—Realist perspective disappears almost entirely. There are differences, to be sure, between *The Common Law Tradition* and some of the glorification of reason, judgment, and common sense that one finds in traditional English celebrations of common law adjudication.[11] And there are differences as well between *The Common Law Tradition* and the more or less contemporaneous Legal Process tradition, which also stressed the importance of reason, judgment, and the rational purposes of law.[12] But these differences are relatively minor when compared to the differences between the paeans to legal and judicial judgment that one finds in Lord Coke, Hart and Sacks, and the later Llewellyn, on the one hand, and the iconoclastic core of the stronger or more extreme Realist perspective,[13] on the other. This more skeptical and perhaps more prototypically Realist position not only plays an important role in *The Theory of Rules*, especially in its earlier chapters and in Chapter VII, but is also one that has more to be said for it, still, than those whose too-easy dismissal (or domestication) of Realism are willing to acknowledge. Much of the modern unwillingness to take a plausible rule-skeptical view seriously has been fostered by some of the rhetorical extravagances in *The Bramble Bush*, as well as by the even less

11. See, most prominently, Edward Coke, *The First Part of the Institutes of the Laws of England* (F. Hargrave and C. Butler, eds, London 1832). A valuable analysis and critique of this self-confident English tradition is Alan Cromartie, *The Idea of Common Law as Custom*, in *The Nature of Customary Law: Legal, Historical, and Philosophical Perspectives* 203 (Amanda Perreau-Saussine and James Bernard Murphy, eds, Cambridge 2007).

12. See Henry M. Hart, Jr., and Albert M. Sacks, *The Legal Process: Basic Problems in the Making and Application of Law* (William N. Eskridge Jr. and Philip P. Frickey, eds, Foundation Press 1995). On the relationship between Realism and Legal Process, see G. Edward White, *The Evolution of Reasoned Elaboration: Jurisprudential Criticism and Social Change*, 59 Va L Rev 279 (1973).

13. In characterizing a strong or extreme Realist perspective, I am not referring to the stylistic extravagances of Jerome Frank, Fred Rodell, or, at times, Thurman Arnold. Rather, I have in mind views closer to the "pretty playthings" position, and thus to the position that canonically inscribed rules, legal texts, formal legal doctrine, and previously decided cases have little (but not no) causal effect on judicial outcomes. For a noncaricatured explanation of this position, see Brian Leiter, *Naturalizing Jurisprudence: Essays on American Legal Realism and Naturalism in Legal Philosophy* 15–118 (Oxford 2007); Brian Leiter, *Legal Realism*, in *A Companion to Philosophy of Law and Legal Theory* 261 (Dennis Patterson, ed, Blackwell 1996). See also Frederick Schauer, *Thinking Like a Lawyer: A New Introduction to Legal Reasoning* 124–47 (Harvard 2009).

guarded statements in Jerome Frank's *Law and the Modern Mind*.[14] It is to be hoped that the publication of *The Theory of Rules* will make the sophisticated but strong Realist perspective on rules, as well as Legal Realism in general, much more difficult to ignore.

Thus, and third, *The Theory of Rules* draws some of its importance from its analysis of the operation of rules in general and legal rules in particular. Apart from what the book adds to Llewellyn's biography and to Legal Realism's historiography, it constitutes an independent contribution, as its title announces, to the theory of rules. At times Llewellyn's analysis of rules in the book may seem clumsy by contemporary jurisprudential or philosophical standards, but a charitable reading yields a harvest of important insights about the relationship between rules and their formulations, between rules and their enforcement, and between rules and their interpretation, while also offering a challenging account of the relationship between legal rules and the nature of law in general.

The Theory of Rules is thus significant for what it tells us about Llewellyn, about Realism, and about rules. The balance of this Introduction, after a brief overview of the contents of the book, will explore each of these themes, with the aim of exposing different dimensions of the context that will enable us fully to appreciate and understand Llewellyn's major but hitherto largely unknown contribution to the literature on legal rules.

I. The Book

The Theory of Rules was planned as a book of ten or eleven chapters, of which Llewellyn had more or less completed eight at the time of his death.[15] But he

14. Jerome Frank, *Law and the Modern Mind* (Brentano's 1930). Among others whose penchant for rhetorical excess has fostered a dismissive attitude about Legal Realism are Thurman W. Arnold, *Institute Priests and Yale Observer—A Reply to Dean Goodrich*, 84 U Pa L Rev 811 (1936); Fred Rodell, *Goodbye to Law Reviews*, 23 Va L Rev 34 (1936). The failure to take Legal Realism seriously has different manifestations. In Great Britain and much of the rest of the common law world, Legal Realism is taught mostly as a joke, or at least as a convenient foil for demonstrating the wisdom of H.L.A. Hart. Excerpts from *Law and the Modern Mind* and *The Bramble Bush* are read and mocked, largely as a precursor to moving on to more serious jurisprudential themes. By contrast, in the United States, it is common for academics to observe that "we are all Realists now"; see Gary Peller, *The Metaphysics of American Law*, 73 Cal L Rev 1151, 1151 (1985); Joseph William Singer, *Legal Realism Now*, 76 Cal L Rev 465, 467 (1988) (book review), while then proceeding to teach and write in a way that ignores most of the important lessons of Realism. Casebooks are still dominated by cases, for example, and still organized according to traditional doctrinal categories, while commentary on Supreme Court decisions criticizes judges whose decisions the commentators object to on ideological grounds as simply making analytical doctrinal blunders.

15. It is highly likely that the manuscript in Llewellyn's papers at the time of his death was the same manuscript as it existed in 1940, for there is no evidence that Llewellyn ever returned

left an outline of his thoughts about the uncompleted chapters, and there is little reason to believe that there was much that Llewellyn wanted to say in this book that was not said in the completed eight chapters, especially because Chapters Nine and Ten appear principally to be elaborations of the themes in Chapter Eight, and Chapter Eleven was envisaged by Llewellyn largely as a summary and conclusion.

Llewellyn seems to have devoted much time and thought to planning the book. We know this in part because of the various outlines he left, and in part because of the way in which the book proceeds by means of a systematic and progressive deepening and elaboration of themes introduced in earlier chapters. Thus, Chapter One is an introduction and overview, establishing at the outset Llewellyn's goal of offering an account of legal rules as inextricably connected with the individuals who interpreted and enforced them, and with the institutions in which they did so. Consistent with Llewellyn's lifelong preoccupation with seeing a rule as something other than, or at least more than, the words on a printed page, his opening chapter seeks to persuade the reader from the beginning that a rule is not just the text of a statute or part of a common law decision, but is rather what the interpreters and enforcers of those texts actually do with it.[16] "Law in action" has always

---

to it after setting it aside. There is thus a plausible claim that *The Theory of Rules* is not a work, especially in this form, that Llewellyn would have published. Whether it is appropriate or desirable to publish works that an author did not (yet) deem publishable at the time of his or her death is an important and fascinating issue, involving intractable questions about the balance between respecting a creator's wishes and respecting the advance of knowledge, about the extent to which a creator's wishes survive his death, and about whether a creator might have preferred publication of an incomplete work to non-publication. Many of these issues arise in the context of the decision, for example, to publish H.L.A. Hart's unfinished "Postscript" to *The Concept of Law* (cited above, note 2), and surface even more commonly in the context of decisions about what do with uncompleted works found in an artist's studio at the time of his death.

16. The point is not novel with Llewellyn, and indeed even Jeremy Bentham stressed the distinction between "the law" and "the statute." Jeremy Bentham, *An Introduction to the Principles of Morals and Legislation* 301 (J.H. Burns and H.L.A. Hart, eds, Athlone Press 1970) (first published 1789). (I am grateful to Stanley Paulson for the reference.) But for Bentham "the law" in this context was the "logical," "ideal," and "intellectual" "whole," which is a far cry from believing, with Llewellyn, that the real rules existed not in overarching or deeply embedded legal principles, but rather in the behavioral inclinations and regularities of rule-appliers, rule-enforcers, and rule-interpreters. If we were to search for the earliest precursors of Llewellyn's concerns, we would look less to Bentham and more to Bishop Hoadly, who famously observed: "Nay, whoever hath an absolute authority to interpret any written or spoken laws, it is he who is truly the Law Giver to all intents and purposes, and not the persons who first spoke and wrote them." Benjamin Hoadly (1676–1761), Bishop of Bangor, sermon preached before King George I (1717), as quoted in John Chipman Gray, *The Nature and Sources of the Law* 172 (Putnam 1909).

been a Legal Realist rallying cry,[17] and from the beginning Llewellyn makes clear that advocates, judges, and institutions are as important to his account of rules as are the naked words with which they deal.

Having foreshadowed the basic theme of the entire book, Llewellyn in Chapter Two attempts to connect his analysis with two of the major jurisprudential themes that were dominant at the time. The first is the understanding of legal rules as commands of the sovereign, an idea with its provenance in Jeremy Bentham[18] and John Austin,[19] and an idea which in 1938 represented a common, and probably the mainstream, jurisprudential ideology.[20] H.L.A. Hart was later to cast much doubt on this understanding of law and of legal rules,[21] but at the time when Llewellyn was writing *The Theory of Rules*, Hart's major contributions were still more than two decades away. In 1938 the Austinian conception of law held sway, and it was a conception to which Llewellyn more-or-less substantially subscribed. In describing legal rules, Llewellyn started from the premise that those rules were commands, and thus were intended and designed by the rule-maker to control, through the use of sanctions, the behavior of others, largely as Austin had elaborated a century earlier. Moreover, Llewellyn expanded the reach of the idea of a command in a way that was reminiscent of (and perhaps influenced by) his contemporary Hans Kelsen.[22] Legal rules were not only commands to citizens, as with the command not to drive a car at more than sixty-five miles per hour on an interstate highway, but were also commands (and, more importantly, empowerments, which is emphatically

17. See Laura Kalman, *Legal Realism at Yale, 1927–1960*, at 9 (North Carolina 1986).

18. Jeremy Bentham, *Of Laws in General* (H.L.A. Hart, ed, Athlone 1970).

19. John Austin, *The Province of Jurisprudence Determined* (Wilfrid E. Rumble ed, Cambridge 1995).

20. John Salmond's *Jurisprudence: or the Theory of the Law* (7th ed, Sweet and Maxwell 1924), had questioned the command account of law well before Hart, but Salmond's challenge had made only limited headway by the time that Llewellyn was writing. Indeed, Edwin W. Patterson, Llewellyn's colleague and friend, had in his 1940 materials on jurisprudence (Edwin W. Patterson, *Jurisprudence: Men and Ideas of the Law* (First Printed Edition, Foundation 1953)) discussed Bentham, Austin, and the command theory extensively (for example, pp. 82–92), but made no mention at all of Salmond's challenge to it.

21. H.L.A. Hart, *The Concept of Law*, cited in note 2; H.L.A. Hart, *Commands and Authoritative Reasons*, in *Essays on Bentham: Jurisprudence and Political Theory* 243 (Oxford 1982). For the view that Hart may have cast somewhat too much doubt on parts of the Austinian conception of law, see Frederick Schauer, *Was Austin Right After All?: On the Role of Sanctions in a Theory of Law*, 23 Ratio Juris 1 (2010).

22. Hans Kelsen, *Pure Theory of Law* (Max Knight trans, California 1967). In 1938 Kelsen's major work existed only in German as *Reine Rechtslehre*, but the German-fluent Llewellyn certainly knew of Kelsen's work, and was both admiring and contemptuous of it. See Twining, cited in note 7, at 499–500.

not the same thing) to judges (and other enforcers of the law). Just as the citizen is commanded not to drive at more than sixty-five, the judge is the "target" of the law that empowers him or her to impose such-and-such a sanction when people are found to have done just what the law says they should not.

Although seeing rules as commands is hardly exclusive to Realism, Llewellyn's attention to prediction, with due acknowledgment of Holmes,[23] is a more characteristically Realist theme.[24] After delving into the question of rules as commands, Llewellyn reorients the discussion to emphasize the human and institutional dimension of rules, and he does so by following John Chipman Gray[25] as well as Holmes in stressing the importance to the lawyer, if not to the judge of a highest court, of being able to predict what a law enforcer or interpreter will do. And thus to Llewellyn figuring out what the rule actually *is* will necessarily involve determining not just what the language of the rule says, but, more importantly, how that language is actually used by those in power. Accordingly, the language of prediction is really Llewellyn's way of emphasizing that for him the rule is what the judges actually apply, rather than how the book of rules actually reads.

Having expressed some sympathy with the command understanding of rules in Chapter Two, Llewellyn devotes much of Chapter Three to moving away from it. He maintains that a rule is a prescription about what ought to happen with respect to some class of conduct, but he then proceeds to insist that what ought to happen, and that what in fact does happen, is rarely a function of a single rule,[26] but is instead a function of a complex array of rules, practices, conventions, professional skills, and, at times,[27] idiosyncrasies, most of which are devoted to trying to achieve a rule's purpose (or "reason"), rather than just following its letter. As Llewellyn puts it, the propositional form of a rule is one thing, what the rule actually does (and,

23. Oliver Wendell Holmes, *The Path of the Law,* 10 Harv L Rev 457 (1897).

24. Although Holmes wrote most famously about law as prediction in *The Path of the Law,* 10 Harv L Rev 457 (1897), he was writing about this theme as early as 1872, and its subsequent propagation by Frederick Pollock prior to 1897 was likely a product of Pollock's reading of and correspondence with Holmes. See Neil Duxbury, *Frederick Pollock and the English Juristic Tradition* 119–27 (Oxford 2004). For an account placing greater weight for the development of a prediction account of law on Pollock and others than on Holmes, see Brian Tamanaha, *Beyond the Formalist-Realist Divide: The Role of Politics in Judging* 72–84 (Princeton 2010).

25. John Chipman Gray, *The Nature and Sources of Law* (Putnam 1909).

26. On the importance of multiple rules to the Realist outlook, see Hanoch Dagan, *The Realist Conception of Law,* 57 U Toronto L J 607 (2007).

27. But only at times. Llewellyn was not Jerome Frank, and was not a particularist about legal decision making even though he believed that many of the nonparticular influences on legal decisions were not to be found in the formal language of a legal rule.

thus, *is*) is another. But although Llewellyn draws this distinction—a distinction central to Realist thought, and to his own contributions to it—he makes clear at the end of the chapter that he is no nihilist about rules or about meaning. He does believe that there is an ideal-type of rule in which the propositional form of the rule is clear in the overwhelming majority of cases, and in which following the propositional form alone will further the rule's purpose and the legal system's function in virtually every instance. But although this is the ideal-type, he says, it is rarely found in practice. Real rules suffer from pathologies of drafting, pathologies of interpretation, and pathologies of enforcement, and thus to locate the real core of real rules we need to look beyond the propositional form to what the relevant legal actors and institutions are doing in actual practice.

With this distinction between propositional form and real rule having been announced, Llewellyn explores and embellishes it in Chapter Four. Using language that will seem to modern readers somewhat misleading, he labels the precise, easily interpreted, and absolute rule a *rule of thumb*.[28] The rule of thumb, he acknowledges, can serve to guide conduct and limit the discretion of interpreters and enforcers, but such rules rarely exist. Moreover, any attempt to create a legal system entirely with such rules will founder on the variability of the human condition and the imperfections of human enforcers and interpreters. Here Llewellyn demonstrates the comparative law competence most prominently exhibited in his *Präjudizienrecht und Rechtsprechung in Amerika*,[29] and takes the occasion to criticize the civil law ideal as embodied by the codes of Frederick the Great and Napoleon. "[T]here is at least one kind of certainty and precision which cannot be had consistently by way of rules of law in a world like Nineteenth and Twentieth Century Europe; and too great an approximation of that kind of certainty and precision comes at an outrageous cost in social discomfort." Thus Llewellyn sees the *elasticity* of the common law and of the round-edged statutes prevalent in the common law world not just as pathologies of poor drafting,

28. The label is misleading to modern readers because in the philosophical and jurisprudential literature a rule of thumb is now understood as a useful heuristic whose strictures should be followed when there is no better information, but which should be ignored when the agent is confident that a different course of action is more desirable. See Frederick Schauer, *Playing By the Rules: A Philosophical Examination of Rule-Based Decision-Making in Law and in Life* (Clarendon/Oxford 1991); J.J.C. Smart, *Extreme and Restricted Utilitarianism*, 6 Phil Q 344, 353 (1956). Thus, the modern understanding of a rule of thumb stresses its lack of strong normative force as a rule, which is just the opposite of the way in which Llewellyn uses the term.

29. Based on a series of lectures Llewellyn gave in Leipzig in 1928, *Präjudizienrecht und Rechtsprechung in Amerika* was published in Germany in 1933, and has now been translated into English. Karl N. Llewellyn, *The Case Law System in America* (Paul Gewirtz, ed, Michael Ansaldi, trans, Chicago 1989).

but instead as a necessary accommodation to a complex and unpredictable world, a world that, at least in Llewellyn's opinion, the classic theorists of the civil law persistently refused to accept.

Recognizing that the idea of elasticity is simply too, well, elastic, Llewellyn turns in Chapter Five to trying to specify both the vehicles of elasticity and the accompanying sources of stability in legal rules. This chapter is simultaneously among the most important and the most elusive, for it is here that Llewellyn attempts to explain, with less than complete success, the way in which legal training, acculturation, and various other dimensions of professional craft serve to move rules away from their literal propositional content while at the same time providing, for sociological and not logical reasons, the degree of stability that Llewellyn was later to label "reckonability." That Llewellyn thought this chapter important is implicit in many of his own marginal notes, but he recognized as well that the ideas still were in need of a better presentation—one that was to come in Chapter Eight—referring to some pages as NSG ("not so good") and scribbling marginal notes to himself on an especially large number of the remainder.

In Chapter Six, Llewellyn deepens these themes, introducing the idea of "situational concepts" that was to play a significant role in his later writings. Again he is not entirely clear about just what a situational concept is, but at numerous places in the chapter he flirts with a strong particularism, suggesting that no two situations are entirely alike, and that the craft of law often involves making the best decision in the full context of a particular case. In later work, and indeed in subsequent chapters of this work, he softens this attitude a bit, talking more about situation-types than situations, but in this chapter of *The Theory of Rules*, there emerges what is not only a prominent Realist theme, but also a theme somewhat in tension with what Llewellyn says about rules and generality earlier in the book.

Much of the early portions of *The Theory of Rules* focus on judges in particular and legal decision makers in general, but in Chapter Seven, arguably the most rule-skeptical chapter in the book, Llewellyn turns from the judge to the lawyer. Here he sees rules as tools that are used by advocates to buttress their desired outcomes, and it is here that Llewellyn, pretty much for the first time, introduces a theme he was to make famous more than a decade later in his penetrating and witty analysis of the canons of statutory construction.[30] In discussing the "advocate's leeway" in *The Theory of Rules*, Llewellyn explains the way in which advocates have various argumentative

30. Karl N. Llewellyn, *Remarks on the Theory of Appellate Decision and the Rules or Canons about How Statutes Are to Be Construed*, 3 Vand L Rev 395 (1950).

devices available to them—modern jargon would call them "moves"—that can be selectively deployed depending on the needs of the moment. Sometimes it is the letter of the rule, but sometimes it is its spirit. Sometimes it is a rule in isolation, but sometimes it is the purpose of a fuller collection of rules. And sometimes it is what a rule seems to require, but at other times it is the larger equity of the situation. Rules are instruments, Llewellyn argues, but instruments in the service of the lawyer's persuasive and argumentative goals, and not nearly as constraining to the good and creative lawyer as the traditional account of rules would have it.

What Llewellyn "grants" in Chapter Seven, however, he takes back, at least partially, in Chapter Eight, which he entitles "Stabilities within the Leeways." Here he distinguishes between desirable legal change, which he acknowledges comes at the cost of some certainty, and erratic change, which has even greater cost and far fewer benefits. But because of these costs, erratic change, he argues, must be cabined by stability. That stability, however, is not, he insists, produced by rules of law. It is produced far more by the craft and mores of lawyers and judges, and by the way in which good lawyers and good judges, disciplined by—and internalizing—the conventions of their roles, maintain a stable system based on the deeper purpose of the law.

It is at this point that the manuscript (mostly) ends. There are fragments of a Chapter Nine on the way in which lawyers and interest groups place pressure on existing rules, and thus on the way in which most legal change takes place within the existing rules rather than by the creation of new ones. Llewellyn's tentative title for this chapter included the phrase "Law My Way," a phrase whose elusiveness is matched by the references in a proposed Chapter Ten to the "Going Whole." And then Llewellyn was intending to summarize the entire book in a chapter on "Rational Rationalization," plainly an attempt to reconcile the core Realist belief that rules often served as ex post rationalizations for results reached on other grounds with his view that rules brought a degree of rationality and stability to what would otherwise appear to be unorganized chaos.

The manuscript as Llewellyn left it is in some sense complete, because it contains largely finished chapters on all of his main themes. But it is also incomplete, not only because the concluding chapters are only fragments, but also because Llewellyn made marginal notes to himself, obviously anticipating further revision. Moreover, there is no reason to believe that Llewellyn did not plan to take account of the numerous marginal comments and challenges from his Columbia colleague Edwin Patterson, a distinguished scholar of insurance and contract law who for many years also taught jurisprudence and whose unpublished teaching materials on jurisprudence were published in 1953.[31] But there is no indication that a manuscript responding or adapting to Patterson's marginalia ever came into existence, so what we have is almost certainly not what Llewellyn would have published had he ever returned to work on this book.

Yet although the manuscript was never completed, even as it stands it represents a substantial contribution to understanding the development of Llewellyn's own thinking, to appreciating without caricature the basic themes of Legal Realism, and to deepening our knowledge of rules in general and legal rules in particular. The balance of this Introduction will examine these themes in turn.

II. The Place of *The Theory of Rules* in the Development of Llewellyn's Thought

There is a tendency among many who have tracked Llewellyn's thought to find strong traces of the moderation and subtlety of *The Common Law Tradition* in Llewellyn's much earlier work, especially in the 1933 *Präjudizienrecht und Rechtsprechung in Amerika*.[32] And a careful reading of his two well-known responses to Roscoe Pound's criticisms of Legal Realism,[33] as well as *The Bramble Bush* itself, confirms that from the beginning Llewellyn did not come close to believing that legal rules were of no consequence.[34]

Yet just as it is important not to characterize Llewellyn solely by reference to law as prediction and to the "pretty playthings" phrase, it is equally important not to domesticate the early Llewellyn excessively. In 1930, in "A Realistic Jurisprudence—The Next Step," he first introduced the idea of a "paper rule," and distinguished paper rules from the "real rules" that he believed described actual judicial decision making. Although Llewellyn acknowledged that the paper rules were "a factor" in determining the real rules that genuinely explained what judges were really doing, that factor had a decidedly subordinate role. It was "rare" for the paper rules accurately to

31. Edwin W. Patterson, *Jurisprudence: Men and Ideas of the Law*, cited in note 20.

32. See especially Twining, cited in note 7; William Twining, *The Idea of Juristic Method: A Tribute to Karl Llewellyn*, 48 U. Miami L. Rev. 119, 124 (1993).

33. Llewellyn, *Some Realism about Realism*, 44 Harv L Rev 1222 (1931); Karl N. Llewellyn, *A Realistic Jurisprudence—The Next Step*, 30 Colum L Rev 431 (1930). Compare Roscoe Pound, *The Call for a Realist Jurisprudence*, 44 Harv L Rev 697 (1931).

34. In 1931, Llewellyn commented that he thought Frank's view of the uncertainty of law was "exaggerated." K.N. Llewellyn, *Frank's Law and the Modern Mind*, 31 Colum L Rev 82 (1931). Much but not all of this view was based on Llewellyn's opinion that lawyerly and judicial craft provided certainty even when rules did not, but some was also based on Llewellyn's belief that legal rules were not quite as inconsequential as Frank and others imagined.

describe judicial behavior, he wrote, and while paper rules sometimes influenced decisions, more often they were either of comparatively little effect or were something to which judges merely paid lip service. The actual effect of the paper rules—the verbal formulas—should be the subject of genuine empirical analysis, Llewellyn argued, but even in this early work he made it clear that he was "skeptical" that the empirical analysis would show paper rules to have much significance in law. It was for this reason, he insisted, that words, rules, and precepts should not be the center of reference for those who were teaching, writing about, or studying law.

Similar views can be found in *Some Realism about Realism*, which was published in the *Harvard Law Review* almost at the same time that *The Bramble Bush* first appeared. And in *Some Realism about Realism*, Llewellyn again made clear that his skepticism about the role of paper rules was significant. Announcing at the outset that he considered Jerome Frank in essence a coauthor of the article, he argued that rule-applying, while admittedly part of what lawyers and judges do, was only a part, and a relatively unimportant part at that. Llewellyn here expressed his "distrust" of the traditional view that written legal rules, whether in statutes or in common law decisions, were very accurate descriptions of what judges were actually doing, or that they were the "heavy operative factor" in producing court decisions. Indeed, he claimed, as he had in *The Bramble Bush*, that "in any case doubtful enough to make litigation respectable," there will almost always be legally legitimate and "impeccable" arguments on both sides. The qualification about litigated cases is vital, but there can be little doubt that throughout *Some Realism about Realism* Llewellyn made clear his agreement with the stronger Realist position that the propositional form of legal rules rarely made a substantial difference in actual litigated or appellate cases.

Llewellyn's scholarly outpouring during the early 1930s was large, and it came during the heyday of Realist enthusiasm. In 1931, a year after publishing *The Bramble Bush*, Llewellyn wrote *Some Realism about Realism* and participated in a *Columbia Law Review* symposium about Frank's *Law and the Modern Mind*. In his contribution Llewellyn distanced himself from Frank's infatuation with psychoanalysis, but otherwise announced that he found Frank's position "essentially sound."[35] Moreover, Llewellyn empha-

35. There is a tendency these days to treat Frank as an idiosyncratic figure whose importance to Realism was marginal. See, for example, Michael Ansaldi, *The German Llewellyn*, 58 Brooklyn L Rev 705, 775–77 (1992); Brian Leiter, *Rethinking Legal Realism: Toward a Naturalized Jurisprudence*, 76 Texas L Rev 267, 268–69, 283–84 (1997). It is certainly tempting to have little patience for rhetorical and argumentative excess and consequently to discount Frank's significance, but that is a mistake. In arguing that the motivations for judicial decisions were different from and

sized again, as he had in *Some Realism about Realism,* his sympathy with the "rationalization" position—the view that legal rules were valuable not so much as decision producing, but rather as the devices that were used to justify or rationalize decisions already made on other grounds.[36]

So although Llewellyn's early 1930s scholarship was more guarded than some have supposed, there is little doubt that he was then closer to many of the allegedly extreme Realist positions than some of the commentators have imagined. Paper rules made a difference to judicial decisions, Llewellyn thought, but not much of a difference, and not often, at least as compared to a large number of human and institutional factors that Llewellyn, along with many of the other Realists of the time, believed were far more causally consequential.

We can thus situate *The Theory of Rules* as an important bridge between Llewellyn's earlier and often less guarded positions, on the one hand, and the later moderate views in *The Common Law Tradition,* and in the *Law in Our Society* materials, on the other. Far more in *The Theory of Rules* than in his later work, Llewellyn emphasizes the gap between the paper rule and the real rule, but far more in *The Theory of Rules* than in *The Bramble Bush* does he begin to elaborate on the non-rule-based sources of stability that were to characterize so much of his writing.[37] Llewellyn did talk of the stability that comes from legal craft even in the 1933 *Präjudizienrecht,* but the discussion there was, even for Llewellyn, especially vague and metaphorical. Yes, the shared craft (and "office") of lawyers and judges could produce predictability (Llewellyn often misleadingly called it "certainty"), he acknowledged, but just how this occurred was not discussed in any depth until the later chapters of *The Theory of Rules.* Even here Llewellyn is far from a paragon

prior to the search for their justifications (and see also Joseph C. Hutcheson, Jr., *The Judgment Intuitive: The Role of the "Hunch" in Judicial Decision,* 14 Cornell L Q 274 (1929)), in discussing the particularistic and fact-specific character of many legal rulings, in stressing the compatibility of formal legal sources with a wide range of results, in recognizing that the personal characteristics of the judge might be relevant to judicial decisions, and in identifying the holistic or gestalt character of judicial behavior, Frank was a pioneer with respect to many important Realist themes that others later developed with more subtlety and qualification.

36. Richard A. Wasserstrom, in *The Judicial Decision—Toward a Theory of Legal Justification* (Stanford 1961), distinguishes the logic of decision from the logic of justification.

37. Although some commentators may underestimate the differences in emphasis and tone between Llewellyn's earlier and later writings, the view that Llewellyn's identification of legal craft as a late life transformation to conservatism (see Morton J. Horwitz, *The Transformation of American Law, 1870–1960,* at 250 (Harvard 1992)), does not stand up in the face of the evidence. Llewellyn was talking about the stability brought by craft and mores as early as 1928, when he first delivered the lectures that became *Präjudizienrecht,* and although these ideas became more prominent in *The Common Law Tradition,* they were plainly part of Llewellyn's thinking from the beginning.

of clarity, and his discussion of shared craft and the constraints of a self-understanding of official position retain more than a small dose of mystery, but at least in *The Theory of Rules* he recognizes that talking about the educational, sociological, psychological, and institutional sources of craft-based and role-based stability and predictability was essential for the success of his larger project.

The Theory of Rules is also an interesting window on Llewellyn's views about statutes and administrative rules. Both *The Bramble Bush* and *Präjudizienrecht* were focused on the common law, and of course so was, much later, *The Common Law Tradition*. But in 1938, when Llewellyn started on *The Theory of Rules*, the statutory enthusiasm of the New Deal was swirling all around him, and in addition he was starting to plan his work on commercial law codification, work that culminated in the Uniform Commercial Code. As a result, we see in *The Theory of Rules* far more attention than elsewhere in Llewellyn's work to statutes, codes, and regulations, and thus to rules, unlike common law rules, that had canonical verbal formulations, what Llewellyn called the "propositional form." And it is here that Llewellyn's view about the gap between those formulations—the paper rules—and the real rules has the greatest Realist bite. The Realist position about the doctrinal indeterminacy of the common law[38] may seem self-evident today, and was hardly totally revolutionary even in the 1930s, but there is a Realist view about the insufficiency of canonically formulated statutory and administrative rules that is substantially more extreme. To say that even an obviously applicable statute does not with its words state the actual rule is hardly the conventional wisdom even now, and Llewellyn in

38. Thus the typical Realist critique of the determinacy of the common law is not very much a claim about the indeterminacy of individual rules. Rather, it is a combination of two arguments. One is that the lack of canonical formulations of common law rules makes it possible to describe and understand them in numerous ways. And the other is that the unsystematic multiplicity of common law rules, principles, canons, maxims, and the like makes it usually possible for the decision maker to find something supporting an outcome reached on other grounds. Thus, common law indeterminacy stems not so much from the individual rules, therefore, as from the largely unconstrained ability of the decision maker to select the rule that she will use. See Andrew Altman, *Legal Realism, Critical Legal Studies, and Dworkin*, 15 Phil & Pub Aff 205 (1986); Felix S. Cohen, *Transcendental Nonsense and the Functional Approach*, 35 Colum L Rev 809 (1935); Felix S. Cohen, *The Problems of Functional Jurisprudence, in The Legal Conscience: Selected Papers of Felix S. Cohen* 77, 83 (Lucy Kramer Cohen, ed, Yale 1960); Walter Wheeler Cook, *Book Review*, 38 Yale L J 405, 406 (1929); Hanoch Dagan, *The Realist Conception of Law*, cited in note 26 (discussing "doctrinal multiplicity"); G. Edward White, *The Inevitability of Critical Legal Studies*, 36 Stan L Rev 649, 651 (1984) ("The Realists demonstrated . . . that for every principle there existed a potential counter-principle").

his observations in *The Theory of Rules* that most (but not all) statutes were some distance away from the actual rules that judges followed made clearer than he did anywhere else that his version of the Realist position was by no means limited to the relatively easy target of the common law.

Llewellyn's writing was always so metaphorical, flamboyant, unsystematic, and opaque that it is easy to find in any of his writings almost all of the themes that emerged at one point or another throughout his career. As a result, those who wish to claim that a concern with both stability and flexibility characterized Llewellyn's entire corpus, from the beginning to the end, will find in almost everything he wrote some support for this claim. But questions of emphasis are important, and there are differences of emphasis and tone between the earliest and the latest work. And that is why it is also possible to trace in Llewellyn's writings a progression from the more strongly rule-skeptical Realist position in much of the work in the 1930s to the more moderate and conventional views embodied in *The Common Law Tradition*. *The Theory of Rules* contains in it support for either of these views about Llewellyn's thought, but it is so substantial a work that it is one that anyone interested in whether Llewellyn's thinking changed from 1930 to 1960, and, if so, how and how much, can no longer be able to avoid.

III. Realism and Rules

So what *is* the Realist view about legal rules, and how, if at all, does *The Theory of Rules* help us to understand it? There is an extreme view, most apparent in Frank's *Law and the Modern Mind*, which understands legal rules as essentially causally inert, having virtually no effect on judicial decision making. This view has two vital components. The first is that a judge's decision on how a case is to come out—the hunch, in Judge Hutcheson's words[39]—is not itself dictated or even guided by legal rules. It might, as Frank thought, be a function of the judge's personal reaction to the parties and the equities of the particular case, or it might, as other Realists believed, be largely a policy decision. But it was not a decision guided by legal rules. And thus the first component of the Realist view of rules is the position that formal rules of law do not have much if any influence on how a judge is initially inclined to decide a case.

39. Joseph C. Hutcheson, Jr., *The Judgment Intuitive: The Function of the "Hunch" in Judicial Decision*, cited in note 35.

Even the most extreme of the Realists, however, recognized the importance of justifying the non-rule-guided decision on traditional legal—rule-based—grounds. Thus, the second component of the extreme Realist position is that the existing stock of legal rules, principles, standards, canons, maxims, and authorities is sufficiently large and multifarious to support virtually any legal outcome. And thus if there is professionally respectable support for a wide range of decisions reached on non-rule-guided grounds, the implication is that legal rules no more constrain than they guide.

When applied to the unsystematic messiness of common law decision making, the extreme Realist view is hardly implausible. And the view takes on added plausibility, as Llewellyn recognized in *The Bramble Bush* and elaborated in *The Theory of Rules*, when it is limited to the set of cases that seem worth litigating and then appealing to parties holding opposed and mutually exclusive positions. We now commonly think of this phenomenon in terms of the *selection effect*,[40] but it was first identified by Llewellyn[41] and received its most extensive elaboration, prior to modern law and economics perspectives, in *The Theory of Rules*. Moreover, the way in which the selection effect makes a Realism limited to appellate cases highly plausible is demonstrated, at the extreme of selection, by the large body of work, mostly by political scientists, on the determinants of Supreme Court decisions. Those determinants, the "attitudinal" position maintains and documents, are rarely the rules embodied in constitutional text or precedents, but are instead the largely non-legal political, social, and ideological attitudes of the Justices.[42] Given that the Supreme Court has in recent years

40. There is a large and growing literature on the selection effect in law, but the seminal article is George L. Priest and William Klein, *The Selection of Disputes for Litigation*, 13 J Legal Stud 1 (1984). See also Richard A. Posner, *Economic Analysis of Law* §21 (3rd ed, Harvard 1986); Frederick Schauer, *Judging in a Corner of the Law*, 61 S Cal L Rev 1717 (1988). An excellent overview of the issues and the literature is Leandra Lederman, *Which Cases Go to Trial?: An Empirical Study of Predictions of Failure to Settle*, 49 Case West Res L Rev 315 (1999).

41. Llewellyn observed that litigated cases bear the same relationship to the underlying pool of disputes "as does homicidal mania or sleeping sickness, to our normal life." *The Bramble Bush*, at 58.

42. As Chief Justice Charles Evan Hughes is reported by Justice William O. Douglas to have said, "At the constitutional level where we work, ninety percent of any decision is emotional. The rational part of us supplies the reasons for supporting our predilections." William O. Douglas, *The Court Years: 1939–1975: The Autobiography of William O. Douglas*, at 8 (Random House 1974). For the empirical research consistent with this conclusion, see, for example, Lawrence Baum, *The Puzzle of Judicial Behavior* (Cambridge 1997); Saul Brenner and Harold J. Spaeth, *Stare Indecisis: The Alteration of Precedent on the Supreme Court, 1946–1992* (Cambridge 1995); Jeffrey A. Segal and Harold J. Spaeth, *The Supreme Court and the Attitudinal Model Revisited* (Cambridge 2004); Jeffrey A. Segal and Harold J. Spaeth, *Majority Rule or Minority Will: Adherence to Precedent on the United States Supreme Court* (Cambridge 2001); Jeffrey A. Segal and Harold

decided on the order of seventy cases a year explicitly selected from the more than nine thousand it is asked to decide, and implicitly selected from the literally hundreds of thousands of litigated disputes in the state and federal lower courts, it is hardly surprising that these seventy are an extremely skewed subset of cases, and a subset virtually defined by the absence of determinative legal authority. In such a domain, therefore, even the most extreme claims of the Realists about the importance of legal rules seem at the very least plausible. And by elaborating more extensively in *The Theory of Rules* than he had in *The Bramble Bush* the nature of the selection effect and the domain in which skepticism about the decision-guiding or decision-constraining capacity of legal rules is most compelling, Llewellyn here both qualifies in an important way the extreme Realist claim about the minimal effect of legal rules, but at the same time makes clear its plausibility within that domain.[43]

As Llewellyn emphasizes throughout *The Theory of Rules*, the Realist view about the consequences of legal rules is overwhelmingly an empirical question. At the heart of the stronger or more extreme versions of the Realist position is the empirical proposition that what Llewellyn called the paper rules have little effect on a judge's determination, especially in appellate cases, of who ought to prevail. And at the heart of the less extreme versions is the claim that the effect of paper rules on judicial decisions still cannot be taken as self-evident, but ought instead to be treated, as Llewellyn insists at numerous places in the book, as an empirical question subject to empirical examination.

In distinguishing paper rules from real rules, Llewellyn did not, Hart's mischaracterization notwithstanding, deny that rules of some sort could have decision-guiding force. It is true that Llewellyn often wished to engage in external descriptive examination in order to determine the actual grounds for judicial decisions. So he would have, for example, applauded an effort to determine the circumstances in which a court would not enforce a written contract for reasons of unconscionability, and he would have expected the

---

J. Spaeth, *The Supreme Court and the Attitudinal Model* (Cambridge 1993); Jeffrey A. Segal and Harold J. Spaeth, *The Influence of Stare Decisis on the Votes of Supreme Court Justices*, 40 Amer Pol Sci Rev 971 (1996). Somewhat more qualified views can be found in Lee Epstein and Joseph F. Kobylka, *The Supreme Court and Legal Change: Abortion and the Death Penalty* (North Carolina 1992); Thomas G. Hansford and James G. Spriggs II, *The Politics of Precedent in the U.S. Supreme Court* (Princeton 2006); Paul J. Wahlbeck, *The Life of the Law: Judicial Politics and Legal Change*, 59 J Politics 778 (1997).

43. And this is why it remains important to recognize the considerable rule-skepticism of even mainstream Realism. See G. Edward White, *The American Law Institute and the Triumph of Modernist Jurisprudence*, 15 L & Hist Rev 1, 34–35 (1997).

result of that research effort to conclude that the circumstances in which contracts were not enforced for reasons of unconscionability departed from what could have been gleaned solely from reading the existing statutes and reported cases dealing with the topic.

To conclude that the paper rules had little effect on the outcome, however, is not to deny the decision-guiding force of rules. Suppose, to continue with the same example, that the empirical examination yielded the conclusion that judges typically and disproportionately found retail consumer credit contracts unconscionable when the seller was a dealer in furniture or automobiles, but not when the seller was a dealer in other goods, and when the contract included time payments, but not when the transaction was entirely in cash. If that were indeed the outcome, it would not, as Llewellyn makes clear in Chapter Four, exclude the possibility that judges had internalized and were guided by and applying a rule making these factors important for the decision.[44] The judges under such a scenario would be applying a rule, but they would be applying a rule other than that written down in the law books. And this is a crucial dimension of the Realist position about rules, especially as put forward by Llewellyn. To be a rule skeptic, or at least a rule skeptic of one sort, is not necessarily to deny that rules guide and constrain the decisions of judges, but is often to maintain that the rules that guide and constrain rule-guided and rule-constrained judges are rules other than the ones located in the words of statutes, reported cases, and legal treatises.

And thus we can now consider the claim that the Realist perspective on rules was excessively dominated and distorted by the view that law consisted of the prediction of judicial decisions. This is a common criticism, but as Llewellyn makes crystal clear, the importance of predicting judicial decisions is a function of the standpoint from which we are examining the effect of legal rules.[45] From the standpoint of the client, the important question is what will happen in court should the client take such and such a course of action. And from this standpoint, the empirical and external prediction of judicial behavior is indeed paramount. If some judge is known persistently, regardless of formal legal doctrine, to side with labor unions in cases in

44. Indeed, H.L.A. Hart is lauded for having distinguished between the internal and external points of view, and for having criticized the Realists for paying attention only to the former and ignoring the latter. But a careful reading not only of *The Theory of Rules*, but also of Llewellyn's 1930 and 1931 writings, shows that Llewellyn understood and set out exactly the distinction that Hart elaborated thirty years later, and that Hart mistakenly accused Llewellyn and the other Realists of ignoring.

45. On the importance of standpoint for this and most other questions of legal theory, see William Twining, *Talk About Realism*, 60 N Y U L Rev 329 (1985); William Twining, *The Bad Man Revisited*, 58 Cornell L Rev 275 (1973).

which employers request injunctions against strikes, then an employer-client will know to act accordingly, and is uninterested, assuming the prediction is empirically sound, in just why that judge decided the way she did.

But Llewellyn plainly recognizes that the standpoint of the client planning a future course of action (or deciding whether to litigate a course of action already taken) is not the only standpoint there is. Both Hart[46] and Dworkin[47] criticize the Realists for not recognizing that arguments to a court or decisions by a court cannot be couched or understood in terms of such predictions. But this is an uninformed criticism. Llewellyn, at the very least, understood that judges can be guided by rules, and that arguments in court can and should be framed in terms of the rules that in fact guide the judges. But to believe that prescriptive rules have a guiding function that law as prediction does not capture is not at all inconsistent with the fact that the rules that guide the judges, and with which the good lawyer might argue her case, are not necessarily the rules that are written in the law books. If judges are known to decide cases of a certain type in favor of labor unions because they believe that it is better policy to do so, they are applying a normative standard, but not the normative standard appearing in the form of a paper rule. The good lawyer, therefore, will try to argue in terms of the normative standard that the judge will actually apply,[48] and will then provide for that judge the legitimating or rationalizing paper rule—the doctrinal "hook"—that the judge can attach, ex post, to the decision reached on different normative or rule-based grounds.

Llewellyn is at the forefront of Realists who argue that the rules that courts apply may not be the rules that are written down on paper, but he is often cryptic about the relationship between the paper rules and the real rules. Although he recognizes that the paper rules rarely represent the real rules, Llewellyn is no linguistic nihilist. He recognizes that paper rules in theory *could* do the work typically expected of them, but he insists as well

46. Hart, *The Concept of Law*, cited in note 2, at 141–47.

47. Ronald Dworkin, *Law's Empire* 36–37 (Harvard 1986).

48. Obviously the extent to which the real rule is the subject of explicit argument will vary with the nature of that rule. If the real rule departs from formal doctrine but is based on policy or the equity of the particular case, few lawyers would be bashful about making policy or equitable arguments. But if the real rule were somewhat less respectable despite its empirical reality—decide in favor of the taxpayer just because the taxpayer is not the government, for example (see Bernard Wolfman, Jonathan L.F. Silver, and Marjorie A. Silver, *Dissent Without Opinion: The Behavior of Justice William O. Douglas in Federal Tax Cases* (Pennsylvania 1973))—than the good lawyer arguing to a judge or court operating in accordance with that real rule will emphasize the taxpayer's status even as she avoids arguing explicitly that such status is a legitimate ground for decision.

that actual paper rules rarely are drafted with sufficient care to serve this goal. Moreover, he recognizes that the pressures of the individual case—the power of the particular—will often inspire judges to want to avoid what appears to be a rule-dictated but erroneous result. In parallel with the views of Jerome Frank, Llewellyn rarely resists the view that succumbing to the power of the particular is both inevitable and desirable, and thus we see his concern with rules that are drafted with sufficient flexibility that they can be interpreted to achieve a rule's underlying purpose.

Llewellyn thus has a view about good rules and bad ones, and does not deny the decision-guiding and judge-constraining potential of good ones. But in drawing the distinction between paper rules and real rules, he lays bare the question—one he rarely addresses except with the occasional oblique suggestion—of the relationship, if any, between the paper rule and the real rule. A contemporary example may make this clear: it is plausible that a Llewellynesque empirical analysis of the real rule that governed the speed of cars on the Massachusetts Turnpike would reveal that the real rule had set the speed limit at seventy-four miles per hour. That is, drivers exceeding seventy-four would be stopped by the police, and those driving at or under that speed would not be stopped, and on the rare occasion when a citation was contested in court judges would impose fines for driving at greater than seventy-four, but would dismiss the case with a warning, or let the driver off on a "technicality," when the recorded speed was seventy-four or less.

This is a typical, even if simple, Realist analysis. There is a rule at work, and one that appears to have been internalized by the police and by judges, and we can get some assistance in finding out what it is by careful empirical examination. And it is not the rule that one would find by looking in the rule book or looking at the posted signs. There is a paper rule, and there is a real rule, and the two are different.

But there is more to the story than this. If "speed limit seventy-four" were the conclusion produced by the empirical research, we would be lax were we not to notice that seventy-four miles per hour is nine miles per hour above the posted speed limit of sixty-five. Sixty-five may not be the real rule, but it—the paper rule—has a causal influence on what the real rule actually is. And if we depart from the crispness of the speed limit example, it might be thought that for many other rules a host of individual and institutional factors would cause the real rule to depart from the paper rule, but in a way that remained connected to the paper rule, such that the real rule could be expected to change if the paper rule were to change. But whether and when this is true is also an empirical question, as Llewellyn recognized. His statements, especially in earlier work, doubting that the paper rule had much influence on the real rule are accordingly most charitably understood as empirical hypotheses that only actual empirical examination could confirm or falsify.

In emphasizing in *The Theory of Rules* the distinction between paper rules and real rules—usually in the language of a distinction between a "rule of law" and its mere "propositional form"—Llewellyn departed from one of the more extreme themes of some Realists, and indeed one to which he occasionally subscribed. In believing that there were real rules, even if not the ones that existed in the law books, Llewellyn signed on to the view that there *were* rules, and, more importantly, that these rules were significant in determining the outcome of litigated and appealed cases. In contrast, however, an important theme of much (but by no means all) of Realist scholarship, and not only in the hands of Jerome Frank and others of his rhetorical ilk, was that legal decision making was essentially particularistic, and that no rule, paper or otherwise, could accurately capture what judges were doing when they decided cases, or could reliably guide judges in making their decisions. Foreshadowing the moral particularism that has surfaced as a frequently debated strand of contemporary moral philosophy,[49] quite a few Realists believed that both the world and the legal decisions about it were so factually and normatively complex that every case was in some important sense unique. Facts were thus very important to these Realists,[50] and although they might have acknowledged that in theory there could exist highly complex descriptive rules that would reflect the complexity of legal decisions, as a practical matter there were so many relevant variables in most legal disputes that any attempt to identify a manageable number of them, whether descriptively or for the purposes of prescription, was doomed to failure.

The Theory of Rules thus emerges as the most important and sophisticated presentation of the Realist position (or positions) on the nature and role of legal rules. It distinguishes between paper and real rules, insists that the relationship between them is contingent and empirical, and ventures

49. See, for example, Jonathan Dancy, *Ethics without Principles* (Oxford 2004); Jonathan Dancy, *Moral Reasons* (Blackwell 1993); Brad Hooker and Margaret Olivia Little, eds, *Moral Particularism* (Oxford 2000); Walter Sinnott-Armstrong, *Some Varieties of Particularism*, 30 Metaphilosophy 1 (1999).

50. Brian Leiter describes the focus on facts, although not necessarily the facts picked out by the written form of a formal legal rule, as a principal component of the core claim of Legal Realism. Brian Leiter, *Naturalizing Jurisprudence: Essays on American Legal Realism and Naturalism in Legal Philosophy* 21–24, 29–30, 109–10 (Oxford 2007).

the opinion that serious testing will reveal that relationship to be much weaker than the traditional understanding would have had it. And, more ambiguously, it sides with Frank and others in identifying the importantly particularistic nature of legal decision making, such that any talk of rules as decision guiding, whether those rules be paper or real, would itself be misleading. At numerous places in the manuscript Llewellyn tempers this Realist view with the praise of the professional craft and the internalization of the professional role that he thought the key sources of legal stability, and on which he relied much more in *The Common Law Tradition*, but there is little doubt that the general picture that emerges is one that is highly skeptical of the role of paper rules and somewhat skeptical of the decisional importance of even the real rules that Llewellyn is at such pains to identify.

IV. *The Theory of Rules* and the Theory of Rules

In many respects *The Theory of Rules* is a far more sophisticated work than those who labor under the common misimpressions of Realism or of Llewellyn might suspect. Its analysis of rules as generalizations, its distinction between descriptive and prescriptive rules, and its understanding of the difference between the guidance and predictive functions of rules are all important contributions to just how we understand what rules are and what they do. Some of these points may seem conventional now, but in the late 1930s they were significant and novel analytic insights.

Most important but also most elusive, however, is the distinction between paper rules and real rules. Llewellyn argues that real rules are the ones actually applied by real officials in real institutional settings, and that as a consequence the real rules diverge in content to a greater or lesser degree from the rules that happen to be found in books or to be otherwise written down. So far so good, but then just what *is* a rule? For Llewellyn it is not, Hart's uncharitable and misinformed criticism notwithstanding,[51] simply an external prediction of decision-maker behavior. Llewellyn understands that a rule is something that decision makers can (but not necessarily do) *use* to guide their decisions. In distinguishing between descriptive and prescriptive rules, Llewellyn demonstrates that he fully grasps the way in which rules have the ability to tell judges and other decision makers what to do,

51. A negative view of Hart's comments on Legal Realism is widely shared, even among Hart's greatest admirers. See, for example, Neil MacCormick, *H.L.A. Hart* 153–57 (2d ed, Stanford 2008).

which is not inconsistent with Llewellyn's Realist point that there is a gap between what a rule tells a judge to do and what a judge actually does.

But if judges at least sometimes and perhaps often do not base their decisions on the meaning of rules as they are written down in authoritative sources—if the rules they use are not the paper rules—then where does the guidance come from? If this guidance is still a rule-based guidance—otherwise why talk of a "real" rule at all?—presumably it comes from a noninscribed rule formulation that nevertheless exists in the mind of the rule applier. Llewellyn is not nearly as lucid as he could be about the source of these real rules, or about the way in which they guide decisions, but he appears to maintain that the real rule that judges (and other legal decision makers[52]) apply is a rule that the judge understands as a rule, and that the judge uses to guide her decisions, but which does not exist in canonical form on a piece of paper.

That there can be such rules should come as no surprise. The rules of language and of etiquette do not have canonical formulations, but exist as rules nonetheless. And thus Llewellyn's belief that legal rules could exist in the same unwritten form should occasion little controversy. In fact, Llewellyn's immersion in common law ideology would make such a conclusion obvious for him, because most of what we think of as common law rules exist without there being a single authoritative canonical formulation. And if it is possible for a rule to exist absent a canonical formulation, it is possible as well that a rule can exist in the vicinity of a similar canonical formulation without being identical to it, which is exactly the principal point of Llewellyn's distinction between paper rules and real rules.

These conclusions seem straightforward, but then the question arises as to whether and when such rules without canonical formulations can serve the purposes we typically associate with rules. When we distinguish rules from standards,[53] for example, and when we identify the circumstances in

52. Unlike many Realists, and indeed unlike much academic commentary on law, Llewellyn appreciated and emphasized the way in which law is located in many places other than the courts, and the way in which law could influence the decisions of citizens and of administrative and law enforcement officials. He began to develop this view in the context of the sociological approach of *The Cheyenne Way*, and in more sophisticated form it became the core of his "law jobs" approach, an approach that was especially prominent in the *Law in Our Society* materials.

53. The literature on the distinction is vast. Among the more useful contributions are Clayton P. Gillette, *Rules, Standards, and Precautions in Payment Systems*, 82 Va L Rev 181 (1996); Joseph R. Grodin, *Are Rules Really Better than Standards*, 45 Hastings L J 569 (1994); Louis Kaplow, *Rules versus Standards: An Economic Analysis*, 42 Duke L J 557 (1992); Duncan M. Kennedy, *Form and Substance in Private Law Adjudication*, 89 Harv L Rev 1685 (1976); Russell B. Korobkin, *Behavioral Analysis and Legal Form: Rules vs. Standards Revisited*, 79 Or L Rev 23 (2000). An influential

which rules might be preferable to standards, we typically believe that the values of stability, predictability, consistency, and constraint on decision-maker discretion are valuable, and that in such contexts the goals of allowing wise and well-meaning decision makers to use their own best judgment to make sound decisions might have to be subordinated to other goals.

When rules exist in the minds of decision makers rather than on paper, however, it is open to question whether these rule-related values can be served effectively. The central feature of a rule, and one especially apparent when rules are compared to standards, is *entrenchment*,[54] the firmly fixed instructions that will resist the urge on the part of an interpreter, applier, or enforcer to avoid the rule in the service of what the interpreter, applier, or enforcer believes the purpose behind the rule to be, or believes the best all-things-considered decision would be. And although rules can be entrenched without their being a canonical written formulation, it seems reasonable to hypothesize that entrenchment is facilitated insofar as a linguistically determinate formulation constrains an individual decision maker's inclination to depart from it. That is, it is likely more difficult in most instances for a decision maker to depart from the meaning of the words on a printed page than to depart from what the decision maker had understood, solely in her mind, the rule to be.

One possibility, therefore, is that Llewellyn's real rules really are rules, and are so firmly entrenched in the minds of judges and other legal decision makers that they operate in pretty much the same ways as canonically formulated rules (sometimes) do. But an alternative and more plausible possibility is that what Llewellyn calls rules are rules only in a softer sense, and that the descriptive regularities they embody are, as he elsewhere applauds, the regularities of craft, of acculturation, and of judges because of their craft often having a shared sense of the purpose of some area of law.[55] None of these sources of regularity is a bad thing, but nevertheless these craft-produced regularities are rule guided only in a weak sense. If we were to empower our police officers simply to "fight crime," but give them no further instructions, it is highly likely that their law enforcement behavior would be systematic and moderately predictable, and that it could be explained in terms of shared values, craft, acculturation, and perceptions of

application of the distinction to some constitutional issues is Kathleen M. Sullivan, *The Supreme Court, 1991 Term—Foreword: The Justices of Rules and Standards*, 106 Harv L Rev. 22 (1992).

54. See Schauer, *Playing By the Rules*, cited in note 28, at 38–76.

55. On Llewellyn's view of the craft of law as being the principal determinant of legal stability and predictability, see Brett G. Scharffs, *Law as Craft*, 54 Vand L Rev 2245 (2001). See also Dagan, *The Realist Conception of Law*, cited in note 26.

social need, but it would be odd to describe the ensuing law enforcement regime as a rule-governed one. And so too with law. The gap between paper rules and observed regularities is not logically inconsistent with there being non-paper rules that are genuinely decision guiding for most judges, but nor is it inconsistent with the observed regularities being a product of something quite different from a rule. The real (descriptive) rules that Llewellyn depicts might be the product of prescriptive rules, but they might also be the consequence of something else entirely.

That the regularities of judicial decision might not be prescriptively rule based is consistent with Llewellyn's normative preference for the rule that wears its purposes or rationales on its sleeve. Yet although Llewellyn devotes much of Chapter Five of *The Theory of Rules* to just such rules, he is rather opaque about what it is for a rule to have this characteristic. More particularly, a rule that announces its purpose—Llewellyn sometimes called a purpose or reason so announced a "singing reason"[56]—might do so in two ways. In one, a rule could be formulated precisely in terms of its purpose. Instead of a "no vehicles in the park" rule designed to minimize noise, danger, and pollution, we might draft a rule that simply said "no noisy, dangerous, or polluting devices in the park." The concerns about such a rule—we would now label it a "standard"—are well-known, and although there are domains in which we prefer standards to rules, the contemporary distinction between rules and standards enables us to recognize that when we opt for a standard we are largely rejecting the constraints of rules, often for good reason.

Alternatively, however, a rule might be formulated with much greater specificity, but yet also, as with the preamble to a statute or a constitution, state what the purpose of the rule was, as an aid to interpretation in hard cases. If it was permissible to make use of that purpose only when the words of the rule were indeterminate—is a bicycle a vehicle for purposes of the "no vehicles in the park" rule?—then announcing the purpose would help reach a correct result in just these kinds of hard cases. But we suspect that Llewellyn has bigger fish to fry. He wants the purpose of a rule to be made explicit so that judges need not apply even the literal words of a rule in cases where such application would be inconsistent with the purposes of the rule. For Llewellyn, as he says on numerous occasions in *The Theory of Rules* and elsewhere, a rule should be applied when and only when doing so would effectuate the purpose for having that rule in the first place.

56. *The Bramble Bush*, at 157; *The Common Law Tradition*, at 183–84.

This sounds eminently reasonable, and it aligns Llewellyn with, for example, Lon Fuller, whose example of the military vehicle embodied in a war memorial was designed to show that applying the words of a rule without reference to purpose was somewhere between impossible and undesirable.[57] But once we see rules as subservient to their purposes, it becomes hard to understand what work the rule qua rule is actually doing. Or, to put it differently, if the purpose trumps the rule in every case in which the rule produces a result contrary to the purpose, then the array of results is extensionally equivalent to the array that would be produced were there no rule at all, and the rule becomes mere surplusage.[58]

Llewellyn's insistence on purpose, therefore, an insistence that encompassed his views about how rules should be interpreted as well as about how they should be drafted, shows him to be at best a fainthearted enthusiast for rules. And this should come as no surprise. A central theme of American legal thought—a core connecting Holmes, decisions like *Church of the Holy Trinity v United States*,[59] the moderate and not-so-moderate Legal Realists, Lon Fuller, the Legal Process perspective, Ronald Dworkin,[60] Guido Calabresi's willingness to apply common law methodology to the interpretation of even precise statutes,[61] and Critical Legal Studies[62]—is a skepticism about taking rules and their formulations too seriously, a skepticism that distinguishes this important and perhaps even defining strand of American legal thought not only from a central aspect of civil law ideology (and perhaps one more crisply and more extremely expounded by Jeremy Bentham

57. See Lon L. Fuller, *Positivism and Fidelity to Law—A Reply to Professor Hart*, 71 Harv L. Rev 630, 661–69 (1958), responding to H.L.A. Hart, *Positivism and the Separation of Law and Morals*, 71 Harv L Rev 593 (1958). See generally Frederick Schauer, *A Critical Guide to Vehicles in the Park*, 83 NYU L Rev 1109 (2008).

58. This conclusion would be otherwise were there a presumption in favor of the rule, such that rejecting the indication of a rule in the service of its purpose required a better reason than would have been required to effectuate the purpose in the absence of the rule. A plausible interpretation of the so-called Golden Rule of statutory interpretation is consistent with this, and would maintain that the literal words of a statute should be applied unless it is very obvious or almost certain that the purpose of the statute would be frustrated by doing so. Under this understanding, there would be instances in which it was possible or even probable (but not certain or highly probable) that applying the rule literally would defeat its purpose, and thus the rule qua rule would retain its decision-guiding force.

59. *Church of the Holy Trinity v United States*, 143 US 457 (1892). See also *United States v Kirby*, 74 US (7 Wall) 482 (1868).

60. Ronald Dworkin, *Law's Empire* (Harvard 1986); Ronald Dworkin, *Taking Rights Seriously* (Harvard 1978).

61. Guido Calabresi, *A Common Law for the Age of Statutes* (Harvard 1982).

62. On some of these connections, see G. Edward White, *From Realism to Critical Legal Studies: A Truncated Intellectual History*, 40 Sw L J 819 (1986).

than by any actual civil law theorist in a civil law jurisdiction), but from the more formal center of legal thinking in most common law countries not located in North America.[63] In stressing purpose over literal meaning, and in distinguishing the paper rules from the real rule, Llewellyn situated himself firmly within this tradition.

An interesting aspect of this tradition is in its treatment of rules. One could describe, defend, and even celebrate the tradition by reference to its frequent avoidance of rules in their strong form. Such an approach would recognize the limitations of rule-based decision making, and would explain and applaud a comparative American willingness to treat rules as having less force than they have in other legal systems, and to employ rule-avoiding devices more frequently than is the case in other jurisdictions. Surprisingly, however, this is not the approach we see from Fuller, from Dworkin, or from Llewellyn, among many others. Rather than acknowledging the potential and contextual difficulties with strong forms of rule-based decision making, they attempt to redefine a rule so that rule-based decision making becomes purpose-based decision making, and in which the difference between rule-generated results and the best or fairest or most just decision becomes the decision generated by this new type of rule. In a way reminiscent of (some) natural law theory's definition of law so as to avoid the possibility of unjust law, what we see here is a (re)definition of a rule that seems almost always to avoid the possibility of an unjust or unfair or silly rule-generated outcome. Ronald Dworkin's defense of the outcome in *Riggs v. Palmer*,[64] for example, does not frame the defense in terms of the deficiencies of following the rule that is the Statute of Wills, but instead argues, as Llewellyn had a half century earlier, that the "real" rule was that combination of statutes, principles, and other norms that together generated a just result. Instead of pointing to the limitations of rules, which are legion, a long tradition, with Llewellyn as one of the pioneers, seeks to redefine prescriptive rules so that they incorporate what are in reality anti-rule perspectives.

Llewellyn tells us a great deal about rules in *The Theory of Rules*. His distinctions between descriptive and prescriptive rules, his analysis of the relationship between a rule and its purpose, his extensive discussion about sources of stability that do not stem from rules, and most of all his distinction between paper rules and the prescriptive rules that judges are actually applying are all substantial contributions to our understanding of the very

63. See Robert S. Summers and Patrick S. Atiyah, *Form and Substance in Anglo-American Law: A Comparative Study of Legal Reasoning, Legal Theory and Legal Institutions* (Clarendon/Oxford 1987).

64. 22 NE 188 (NY, 1889).

idea of a legal rule. But it is important to take the title of the book with a grain of salt. What Llewellyn provides for us is not the theory of rules, but rather Llewellyn's theory of rules, a theory of rules that turns out to be a theory or account of the weaknesses and limitations of rules. This descriptive account of rules embeds for him an account of how often, especially in the United States, the weaknesses and limitations of rule-based decision making have led lawmakers to avoid using rules, and have led judges to look for ways to circumvent them. Even without the examples that Patterson's handwritten marginalia incessantly prod Llewellyn to provide, Llewellyn accurately captures and celebrates a characteristically American approach to rules, and in doing so provides powerful evidence of why he remains such a central figure in American legal thought.

EDITOR'S ACKNOWLEDGMENTS

This endeavor owes much to Professor William Twining. It was Twining who first located and catalogued Karl Llewellyn's unpublished manuscript on rules,[1] and it was Twining's references to the manuscript in his own important work on Legal Realism[2] which initially prompted me to read the manuscript and conclude that it should be made available in published form. Twining has encouraged me throughout this project, even though our understandings of Llewellyn's lessons at times differ.

Judith Wright, director of the Law Library at the University of Chicago Law School, was uncommonly helpful in locating the manuscript, making it available for my use, and securing permission for its publication. At a later stage of the project, Sabrina Sandhi of the Columbia Law Library provided valuable assistance with manuscripts by Llewellyn's colleague, friend, and commentator Edwin W. Patterson. And Barry Cushman, Bobbie Spellman, G. Edward White, and Kenneth Winston offered helpful suggestions and references.

The editor's Introduction was presented as a faculty workshop at the University of Virginia School of Law, where my colleagues were typically helpful and constructively critical, and again at the School of Law of Washington University, where again the audience comments provided valuable insight and correction. The Introduction also benefited from the comments of Hanoch Dagan, Neil Duxbury, Jeffrey O'Connell, Stanley Paulson, Torben Spaak,

1. William Twining, *The Karl Llewellyn Papers* (Chicago 1968).

2. William Twining, *Karl Llewellyn and the Realist Movement* (Weidenfeld and Nicolson 1973, reprinted with Postscript, 1985).

and Brian Tamanaha, and the project was supported throughout by funds first from the Harvard Law School and then from the University of Virginia Law School Foundation.

Frederick Schauer
Charlottesville, Virginia
April 2010

EDITORIAL NOTES

All material in brackets was provided by the editor, and a set of empty brackets in the text is an indication that a word or words were moved or removed to make the text more readable. Material not in brackets is exactly as it appears in Llewellyn's typescript, and I have made no effort to update Llewellyn's style, syntax, or punctuation. Thus, the pronouns and examples remain all male, commas usually appear outside of quotation marks, italics are overused, and many of the sentences and paragraphs are excessively long. Indeed, the reader who finds Llewellyn's writing idiosyncratic and sometimes difficult to follow will not be alone, and it sometimes appears as if Llewellyn strained too much to make his style literary or poetic. Few people other than Llewellyn, after all, could have imagined that the words "English" and "ostrich" could be used as verbs. At other times, his use of language, especially prepositions, was unusual even for his time, and the reader will find little rhyme or reason to Llewellyn's choice among, for example, "in," "on," "to," and "with."

The existing typescript contains some marginal handwritten comments by Llewellyn himself and many by his Columbia colleague Edwin W. Patterson. Where Llewellyn's comments take the form of specific changes in the text, I have made the changes that he plainly wished to be made, but I have not attempted to make any nonspecific changes that Llewellyn expected to make in the future, such as where he commented to himself that a sentence or paragraph was unclear. And although I have not included any of Patterson's marginalia, it is worth noting that his comments demonstrate the admirable efforts of someone to put himself inside a colleague's project and mindset, even if he did not share the project's overall perspective.

The manuscript contains no footnotes, and thus all footnotes have been added by the editor. Citation format for the footnotes and in the editor's Introduction conform to the *University of Chicago Manual of Legal Citation*.

The Theory of Rules

History and Acknowledgments

The preparation of this book began, I suppose, when in working up a course on American case-law for use in 1928 at Leipzig I first read cases with an eye less on what they decided than on what they were doing with the rules which had antedated the case at hand. Since then I have been exploring aspects of the matter, in my *Präjudizienrecht*,[1] in various papers on phases of Sales and Contracts, in unpublished studies on the technique of legal argument and on one criminal cause célèbre,[2] in studies of legal education and of the bar and its work. The present volume took form around the challenge to the nature and work of rules in general and in our system in particular which was presented by [Edwin W.] Patterson's stimulating outline for the undergraduate law course in Jurisprudence at Columbia Law School.

I have some hesitance in attempting more particular acknowledgments. There are no statements in the book which I do not believe to be obvious, or which ought to have their obviousness cluttered by reference to "authority." There are no lines of thought which do not seem to me common property of the trade. I have sometimes referred to a particular author when some phrasing of his happened to cross my mind as I wrote; but it might as well have been Max Radin or [Arthur] Bentley as [Roscoe] Pound or [John] Dickinson, if it chanced to be Pound or Dickinson, and it might as well have been a proverb or a nobody or a line from Shakespeare, or any other phrasing which happened to be happy and to my point. I think I have probably drawn from [Arthur L.] Corbin, Walter Wheeler Cook, Max Weber,

1. [K.N. Llewellyn, *The Case Law System in America* (Paul Gewirtz ed, Michael Ansaldi trans, University of Chicago Press 1994)].

2. [Llewellyn had actively assisted and publicly advocated for the defense in the Sacco and Vanzetti trial in 1928.]

study of Erwin Griswold's arguments, from a paper of [William Draper] Lewis' and from the critiques of my prior writing by L.L. Fuller and Eugene Ulmer, more frequently and more directly. But most of the direct stimulus has come from mulling over the opinions, and most of the correction of off-center seeing has come from the students in my seminar.

For huge help in the phrasing and in getting clear the bearing of semi-inconsistent part-truths on one another, I am grateful to those who have lavished time on the manuscript, notably E.W. Patterson,[3] Henry Harfield, Soia Mentschikoff[4] and Emma Corstvet.[5]

K. N. Llewellyn
Columbia University Law School

3. [Edwin W. Patterson, Llewellyn's colleague at Columbia and a prominent scholar of contracts, insurance, and jurisprudence, made extensive marginal comments on the entire manuscript. Llewellyn gratefully reciprocated, and the drafts of Patterson's contracts treatise contain extensive notations by Llewellyn.]

4. [Soia Mentschikoff was Llewellyn's colleague at Columbia, his major collaborator on the Uniform Commercial Code, and his wife from 1946 until Llewellyn's death in 1962.]

5. [Emma Corstvet was a research assistant to Underhill Moore at Yale, and married Llewellyn in 1933.]

CHAPTER I

The Frame of the Discussion

Prelude

When lawyers speak of "the law," the[y] mean sometimes, and a touch vaguely, the net effect of our legal institutions on a case or situation. But more often, and always when it gets down to more accurate discussion, they mean some *rule* with official status and authority, one which can claim official application in the courts. They mean a rule which already has been or with proper care and skill can be cast into words, and read for the meaning which the courts will give it, a rule which proper care and skill can determine to be *the* rule covering the case or problem in hand. Such is "the law" which lawyers tell a client "is in his favor", is "clear"; or is "not settled"; [or] is "clear enough, really, but not safe to rely on in the present temper of the court"; [or] is "very satisfactory on this" or is "outrageous."

Lawyers as lawyers do not often bother to state or even to figure out just what they mean by a "rule"; and things they refer to as "rules" may have widely variant form and content.[1] But pretty commonly implicit in any reference to a "rule" are a number of elements which jurisprudes[2] and

1. [In noting that the one word "rule" may refer to ideas or concepts with "widely variant form and content," Llewellyn tracks the Realist precursor Wesley Newcomb Hohfeld, who analyzed the different but interlocking relationships to which the word "right" commonly referred. Wesley Newcomb Hohfeld, *Fundamental Legal Conceptions Applied in Judicial Reasoning* (W.W. Cook, ed, Yale 1919).]

2. [Scholars of jurisprudence have different views about what to call themselves. Europeans commonly use the term "jurist," but to American ears the word seems to refer as much if not more to a judge as to a writer about legal theory. Some English-speaking legal philosophers prefer the label "jurisprudent," which dates back to Coke in referring to anyone learned in the law. But Llewellyn's "jurisprude," which he appears to have coined, has become common. And not only does "jurisprude" specifically designate a scholar, but it also carries an admirable absence of pretentiousness.]

logicians have sorted out for observation, some of which it pays to look at early. A "rule" is general, and not limited to one person or occasion.[3] A rule ought to be in clear explicit language, and if the rule is really clear, it is or can be put in such language.[4] That language indicates in general terms some fact-situation, and it indicates some "legal consequence" of any such fact-situation. The "legal consequence" is a designation, immediately or remotely, of what a legal official (normally a judge) is supposed to do when he is in proper fashion confronted with proper indication that some state of fact falling within the rule has been presented to him for action. Implicit in a "rule" is a command to any relevant official to act under and according to the rule;[5] and unless the contrary is suggested, there is implicit in any statement that the rule is [a] "clear" [ ] prediction that the relevant official will act as he thus officially *ought* to. When he acts, the organized power of the State will back his action. But part of the idea of "*legal*" consequence is not only that such official action is proper and often officially mandatory, but that the range and degree of such action is also *limited*. The action will be, say, fining, not hanging; imprisonment for one year, not for twenty; levy for three hundred dollars and forty cents, not for ten thousand.

Such is the type of thing lawyers have in mind when they speak of "the law" of a case; and the vast sum of all such rules for all the types of case covered by the law is to lawyers "the law" of a State; and the law books are the books out of which "the law" in this sense is to be gathered. With

3. [The distinction between particular and general prescriptive language—between a command to do *this* on *this* occasion and an order to take actions of some type whenever circumstances of some type arise—is developed with care in John Austin, *The Province of Jurisprudence Determined* (Wilfrid E. Rumble, ed, Cambridge 1985)(1885), and analyzed extensively in Frederick Schauer, *Playing By the Rules: A Philosophical Analysis of Rule-Based Decision-Making in Law and in Life* (Clarendon/Oxford 1991).]

4. [Here Llewellyn tracks the now ubiquitous distinction, probably attributable originally to Roscoe Pound, between relatively clear and precise *rules* and more vague and indeterminate *standards*. See Frederick Schauer, *Thinking Like a Lawyer: A New Introduction to Legal Reasoning* 188–202 (Harvard 2009); Clayton P. Gillette, *Rules, Standards, and Precautions in Payment Systems*, 82 Va L Rev 181 (1996); Joseph R. Grodin, *Are Rules Really Better than Standards?* 45 Hastings L J 569 (1994); Louis Kaplow, *Rules versus Standards: An Economic Analysis*, 42 Duke L J 557 (1992).]

5. [Llewellyn's understanding of all rules as commands, even if in some cases as commands to officials and not to rule subjects, owes much to Austin and, with respect to legal rules as (in part) commands to officials, to Hans Kelsen (*Reine Rechtslehre*, 1928, subsequently translated into English as *The Pure Theory of Law* (Max Knight trans, California 1967)), the works of each being very familiar both to Llewellyn and to the jurisprudential culture of the late 1930s. The well-known criticism of reducing all legal rules to commands of some sort is in H.L.A. Hart, *The Concept of Law* (Penelope A. Bulloch and Joseph Raz, eds, 2d ed, Clarendon/Oxford 1994).]

these "positive" or actually prevailing rules lawyers often contrast or compare "justice", reminding the layman that whenever the positive rules are not just, then courts are "courts of law and not courts of justice". With these "substantive" rules which lay down the proper official result of given types of fact-situation lawyers contrast "procedural" rules (which are also rules of law, but rules looking only to getting official results with and out of the "substantive" rules which give men legal "substantive" "rights" and "duties"); and they may tell a client that his *right* is clear under the law, but that his *remedy* is worthless or expensive or difficult or uncertain. That means that a full and accurate statement of "the rule" covering his case is really much less favorable than a shorthand and inaccurate statement which hides the hurdles and difficulties in the way of getting his facts *properly* before a proper official, or which hides limitations vital to the client on what the official is supposed to do. This is important to us because it indicates how widely the degree of accuracy and articulation can vary among the things which lawyers treat as "rules of law"; just as the comparison with "justice" indicates how thoroughly-limited "the law" can be to what it just happens to be, in temporary utter disregard of what it may be for. And the fact that a lawyer may see "the law" as clear, but yet raise doubts as to what the officials will do about it, unless he can "get it before Judge Brown", reminds us that "the law" is not self-operative, in the pinch, in regard to the "legal consequence" the rule lays down; that "legal consequence" is an officially stated "should be", but in the pinch it can be translated into "isness" only through a human being in office. The further fact that the lawyer may find "the law" to be uncertain or unsettled or to be not clear, although we know that if a question is properly presented to a judge he *has* to *do* something clear about it, reminds us again of the human element in the picture. For if "the law" is to be clear, somebody or some body must first have made it clear; and even if it is not clear, a person or persons in the shape of a court acting "under and according to the law" must, when properly appealed to, take some action which will render more clear in the future the same "law" which has failed to get clear beforehand. Finally, the lawyers are all agreed that digging "the law" out of the books of law is something of an art. The untutored layman will have his troubles doing that. Indeed, lawyers agree that lawyers differ among themselves in the skill and accuracy with which they accomplish such digging. Moreover, judges are also lawyers, and are also lawyers of unequal ability, and judges are helped and counsel[ ]ed in their search for and determination of "the law" by other lawyers, again of uneven ability.

From this is would seem to follow that in the determination of what "the law" is and means in any cause, the lawyers themselves recognize the influence of factors additional and supplementary to such "rules of law" as we have been discussing. One type of such factor is, obviously, something in the nature of professional lawyer's techniques, whose possession marks the lawyer off from the medic or the structural steel worker or the housewife—from all laymen. Another type of factor would seem to be the personal skill, intuition, artistry, or thumb-fingeredness and obtuseness, of particular individuals at the bar and on the bench. Certainly, there is something of the trade about the determination, and there is something of the individual about it; and I think no lawyer will claim that we have "rules" which fully and satisfyingly cover and guide and control either of these somethings. Indeed, most lawyers will tell you that one main office of the "rules of law" is to reduce *so far as possible* such variations as must occur in the working out of these other two somethings. And, with a sigh or a grin, they will point out that in practice they find that "so far as possible" reaches by no means far enough to make things run in disregard of the person; that the good ones are good, though even a good one has his kinks; while the bad ones are pretty sour, but not all sour the same way; and there is indeed a lot more than "the law" to the practice of law.—Meantime, it will take a cynic of unusual lack of balance to disbelieve that at least many of the officials, where "the law" of any case before them is not crystal clear, allow an ideal of what good law for that situation might be to influence the touch of shaping which they proceed to give to "the law" by their decision and action. And even the most psychopathic of cynics, squinting all things in terms of lowest motivation,[6] will have to admit that to give effect to a low motive in decision, a judge would still have to give his result some advance idealization in the form of a projected picture of how his decision might better serve the common woe.

The resulting picture seems clear and straight enough, and it ought to look to a layman when he thinks about it much as it looks to a lawyer when the lawyer stops to look at it.

First, we have rules of law, lots of them, some very clear, some not so clear, some exceedingly unclear. In the measure of their clarity, they make possible, in the classes of case they cover, the arrangement of official action

6. [Llewellyn wrote "clear?" in the margin at this point, perhaps because the phrase "lowest motivation" seems ambiguous as between, at least, the "low motivation" of a judge who wishes to disregard the rules of law to reach the most equitable result in a particular case, or the even lower motivations of a judge who had a personal preference for one of the parties or who wished to reach the result that would most benefit his judicial career and reputation.]

with precision and in independence of the person.[7] Even where unclear to a layman, they may be so built that the most ordinary techniques of the lawyer's trade will make them clear to any lawyer. Rules like that plainly have an important function to perform in our society. They help tremendously in our predicting of official action, in our knowing what action laymen are officially expected to take, in our planning lay action and trimming lay sails to make the official wind drive the boat along. They help to control official action; a standard against which improper action by officials can be detected, and corrected, or castigated. It is easy to see why men like the idea of a whole regime of such rules—so much so as to sometimes talk and think and emote as if all our rules were that sort of fine clear rules, and as if we had in consequence a government wholly "of laws" and not at all "of men." With such rules before the eye as being what "*a* rule of law," *any* "rule of law" is, it is also easy to see why "the rules" loom so large in lawyers' thought as to constitute in much of their thinking, "the law", all of "the law"; and to see why study of "the law" is given over so largely to study of the rules; and why when things do not go to suit, one of the first thoughts can be to pass a law about it: a new rule, a clear rule, a rule of this ideal type.

But, second, and equally, it is plain that not all the rules are so clear as this, even to lawyers or to judges and administrators. Indeed it is interesting, when one more closely watches the training of the prospective lawyers, to discover how much of that training goes to technique of *trying* to get a clarity out of the available books which those books do not offer in any simple accessible form; and it is even more interesting to discover how unevenly those techniques are in fact learned, and even taught; and how largely also they are *inarticulate*, techniques not available to ready communication; and, whether they are articulate or just *ways* of doing the work, to be "picked up", how largely the techniques are inconsistent with each other. Not all the rules, I say, nor all the lawyer's trade techniques of work on them, are ideally clear.

Yet rules, as aforesaid, are often clear to lawyers, as to their application, their effect, their range, which are not at all clear to laymen. Now this can only mean that *to some important extent* the trade techniques take hold of the rules and shape their meaning to persons of the trade. Lawyers somehow

7. [Discussion of "the rule of law" was widespread in the late 1930s, as it is now, and Llewellyn's reference to official action "in independence of the person" calls forth the idea embedded in the common distinction between the "rule of law" and the "rule of men," a distinction that Llewellyn will note later in this paragraph.]

get so that they get meaning out of language which other men do not get; to an important extent they get very similar meaning, among themselves. In the language of the sociologist, the lawyers have become the personnel of an *institution*; they have become broken into *ways* of doing, *ways* of talking, *ways* of thinking, *ways* of feeling, which are transmissible to new personnel. And *never* is the transmission of the ways which make up an institutional pattern *wholly* by way of conscious instruction, still less *wholly* by way of formulated rules in any handbook or set of regulations. Some of the transmission just happens—it happens by association and imitation, by haphazard correction and advice, above all, by *doing* the work, by getting "the hang of it". Again, never is any *complex* institution capable of breaking in new personnel with the identity of resultant reaction once achieved by Mr. Tillen's dancing girls.[8] Not even old Japan accomplished such a uniform shaping of men; the scattered multiform training of American lawyers certainly does not.

We are left, then, with a range both of great uniformity *and* of openness to material variation within the field "covered" by the rules of law themselves. We are left, secondly, wherever the rules fail to have been formulated with crystal clarity, again both with a field of prospective uniformity and a field of prospective variation in the understanding and the action of lawyer-personnel and of judge-personnel and of other official personnel. We are left, by consequence, with a government both of laws *and* of men; a government which ranges from utter predominance of the first, through degrees of mixture in which individual variation becomes more and more important, on into spots where the most vital factor in the case will be the idiosyncrasy of the particular official. We are left with a rationalized and articulate framework of rules which *aims* at elimination of such idiosyncrasy, but which makes the grade only in part. We find that the rationalized and articulate framework is partly but not wholly implemented and supplemented by less rationalized and above all less articulate institutional machinery which is the engine for accomplishing much regularity which the less neatly articulate of the rules fail, in themselves, to achieve. We must find, within the leeway that is left, that officials govern their actions at least in part by ideals about a good society and about a better law, and by forward projection of generalizations about the future use of any decision as a guide—as being in effect, though perhaps not in intent, creative of *new* law. And, turning back to the framework of our rules, we can see that each of those rules came into

8. [The reference is to the Radio City Rockettes, a troupe of dancers whose performances were characterized then, as now, by the perfectly coordinated precision of their movements.]

being by way of one man's judgment, or of many men's judgments, or of the successive judgments of many men, about what ought to be "the law" of a situation—whether such "ought judgments" were directed to the commonweal or to their own. Aspiration of some kind went into the making of those rules, and so did imaginative forward-projection of some minds upon at least some parts of what the results of any rules would be, or even upon plans to which a rule became a deliberate tool.

All of this fits into a general pattern not too hard to state and to see. There are yearnings and aspirations, there are vaguely or clearly envisaged idealizations of conditions which might be made to be, there are purposes in sunset cloud or mental blueprint. To these any relevant rule or rule-structure is related as means relate to ends. A means is to be appropriate, a means is to be effective. A *chosen* means is not only a tool but a limitation. If it is inappropriate, its very effectiveness is a crippling of its end. Thus with the rules of law. They are measures, measures to be judged against their purposes. But once called into being, they are also limitations on effectuation of any purposes which do not fit the actual form and nature of the rules.[9] Their "purposes", moreover, are not the simple relatively single purposes of a bachelor farmer planning his kitchen garden. Their historical or genetic purposes are mined of many men and many motives; their emergence is also commonly not at one stroke, but drags over a changing stretch of time, with the men and the purposes of the men concerned shifting and changing in the process. Though the purpose-means pattern of idea is simple, the pattern of the weaving is bafflingly complex. Yet there results, in any rule or body of inter-related rules, a type of to All-of-us, a type of net purpose which must be figured out if the rule is to have meaning beyond the flat fiat or fact that "Thus it is." Let me repeat, moreover, that unless the rule, and all of a body of inter-related rules taken together, and also the net meaning of the whole of them on any point within their purview, has been made clear as a mountain pool in wind-still sunlight, then fresh idealizations not

9. [This is a remarkably traditional and, indeed, non-Realist, statement about the force of rules, especially from someone who less than a decade earlier had referred to rules, albeit casually, as "pretty playthings." Now Llewellyn appears to be saying that a rule cannot be interpreted to serve its background purpose when the language of the rule precludes such an interpretation. In reaching this conclusion, Llewellyn sets himself at odds from the strong purposivists of later generations, theorists such as Lon Fuller, Ronald Dworkin, and Guido Calabresi, all of whom concluded that American law frequently and properly sets aside even the clearest of statutory language when following that language would frustrate the background purpose of the rule. See, for example, Guido Calabresi, *A Common Law for the Age of Statutes* (Harvard 1982); Ronald Dworkin, *Law's Empire* (Harvard 1986); Lon L. Fuller, *Positivism and Fidelity to Law—A Reply to Professor Hart*, 71 Harv L Rev 630, 661–69 (1958).]

found in the words of the rules are entering constantly into the shaping of the *meaning* of the rules.

But again, these rules which in relation to "purposes" can be seen only as measures, turn as against what we may call their effects into purposes themselves. In whatever form they are, to their own legal system they are given things intended to control. They are intended to control and arrange and coordinate the behavior of laymen. Words—and rules use words as their primary machinery—can effect such results only by passing through *men* trained and shaped into teamplay and institutional patterns, to act through those men upon other men trained and shaped, no less, but shaped into other teamplay and into other institutional patterns. The very impact of language or of gesture upon us is a thing of teamplay: no single person makes or speaks a language, or gives conventional meaning to a sign. Into the given institutional machinery which society at any moment possesses—or of which, if you prefer it, society at any moment largely consists—the rules of law are fed; and not only do the rules produce effects as they stir that machinery, but the machinery also shapes and reshapes the rules, to the extent that the rules, as they go in, are loose of edge and substance.[10] It takes a hard rule, a well-made rule, compact, clean of outline, definite and sure of scope and detail, and built to a feasible end, to pass through the institutional machine and come out still its original self, still wholly master of its destiny and indeed of its meaning. Some rules accomplish this. Even some whole sets of rules accomplish it in large part. Some rules do not accomplish it. Some are blunted or distorted out of recognition; some are shunted in to practical discard. I want to be very certain that I am no[t] understood, in this, as saying merely that lazy or willful or corrupt administrators sometimes are found who do not obey the law. For what I am saying, though it can be developed to cover also the problem of culpable distortion or neglect of rules by any official, is not directed at such abuse at all. It is directed to the reshaping by our professional institutions and personnel of the effective, positive, prevailing *meaning* of the very rules by which the correctness of official behavior is, and is to be, adjudged. In the process of becoming a rule, *prevailing* and *authoritative*, any would-be rule is *read* into, and read through the prisms of, the institutional structure of the going lawways and of the existing lawmen; and unless it is a peculiarly well built form of words

10. [Again Llewellyn implicitly distinguishes the "loose" rule, whose language makes the rule malleable, from the tight rule, whose precise language makes malleability far more difficult, if not impossible. And thus he again makes clear that, for him, legal indeterminacy may be less a function of the necessarily indeterminate nature of rules or of language than of the indeterminate rules that, contingently, dominate the American legal landscape.]

with a peculiarly well designed sense, the rule is modified and even made over in that process. This is what lies at the core of [John Chipman] Gray's insistence that not the legislature but the court of last resort *made* "the law" of a statute,[11] or of a court's ruling that statutory language is to be given common law definition, or that "a change so radical would surely have been put in more explicit language"; but those are colorful dramatic instances, whereas the process I speak of does its heaviest work in unperceived pervasive quiet.

Thirdly,[12] just as purposes are not always clean-limbed, and just as rules may be either sharp or vague, so the interlocking patterns of action, thought, and conjoined feeling [,] which I have referred to as institutions, have grown to be now tight and compulsive, but again will be discovered in groping emergence or in uneven decay. No court, today, would look at a constitutional statute and flatly disregard it; the pattern there is tight. But whether an ancient and offensive anomaly popping up after fifty years is to be dealt with as plainly out of line with modern principle and so discarded, or is to be dealt with as too firmly settled to disturb, that is not a matter on which our institutional patterns can be seen as fixed. Where rules or institutions offer alternative patterns, or offer none with clarity, there is much leeway for individual variation; there is no high degree of "control" nor of prediction which does not reckon with the person.

All of this is so obvious that there might seem no point to the saying of it. After looking the situation over this way one does not readily see how a thoughtful student of jurisprudence can find it useful to define law as commands, and commands alone;[13] or urge that the law is made of decisions *and not* of rules;[14] or consider it as constituted of normative propositions,

11. [In *The Nature and Sources of Law* (Putnam 1909, 2d ed, 1921), Gray famously distinguished law from the sources of law, arguing that statutes were only sources of law and not law itself. For this and other reasons, Gray is often taken to be one of the important precursors of Legal Realism.]

12. [It is not clear what are the first and second components of this argument, nor was it to Edwin Patterson, whose marginal notes on the manuscript asked about the identity of the first and second items.]

13. [Llewellyn is referring to the dominant jurisprudential view of his time, the so-called command theory of John Austin, as set forth in *The Province of Jurisprudence Determined,* first published in 1837, and cited above, note 3.]

14. [The likely referent is Gray, cited in note 11, although it is interesting that here Llewellyn also distances himself from a common conception, or misconception, that Legal Realism can be reduced to the claim that law is the prediction of judicial decisions.]

and of nothing else[15]—still less how anyone can consider it as made up exclusively of such propositions already cast into clear verbal form. Nor does one at once understand how thoughtful men can come to talk either as if "the rules of law" gave us certainty of decision; or as if they gave us all such certainty of decision as we have; or as if they had no part or no important part in regularizing decision and making it often certain.

What gives some understandability to the writing and thinking of such queer positions as those mentioned is recollection of the fact stated at the outset of this chapter: when lawyers talk of "the law", meaning the impact of the going legal system as a whole, they *feel* themselves to be talking *loosely* (however sensibly). On[e] of the parts of their institution is, when they take thought and begin to talk "with accuracy and care", that they must and do confine the idea "law" to authoritative rules. One of the parts of their institution is that their *official* talk, in court and to judges, or in books "of law", must deal with rules, and with rules phrased in words, as stating "the law", and that anything else, whether it be "the purpose" of a rule or of a body of rules, or the "practice and understanding of the profession", or "the manifest justice of the case", must be treated as being something else than "the law".[16]

There is a solid core of sense in this convention. In the first place, the office of rules of law is to control official behavior. If there is a rule to be had for the purpose, that rule needs to be called into play, and when called into play, it is to govern. The convention requires that any rule there may be, be looked for, and the convention furthers the conduct of that search with care. That has virtue. In the second place, a really well-drawn rule, skillfully tailored to a clear and feasible purpose, *will* control the official behavior of any but a flagrant official, and it will hugely aid in checking up on such an one.[17] The convention, in keeping this demand made on rules to the fore, has its

15. [The reference in the text is probably to Hans Kelsen, cited above, note 5, whose *Reine Rechtslehre*, later translated as *Pure Theory of Law*, was widely discussed in the 1930s, was plainly accessible in the original German to Llewellyn, and whose claims resemble those that Llewellyn notes here.]

16. [In a marginal note to himself, Llewellyn indicated that he thought this paragraph contained two separate ideas, one about the difference between the law and authoritative rules, and the other about the way in which the internal or official talk of lawyers and judges is largely the talk of authoritative rules only. H.L.A. Hart, in *The Concept of Law*, cited above at note 5, famously charged the Realists with ignoring the "internal point of view" of participants in the legal system, but it is clear from this passage that Llewellyn well understood the difference between an external descriptive standpoint and an internal one that spoke *from* and not just *about* legal rules.]

17. ["An one" seems dissonant to modern ears, but was somewhat more common when Llewellyn was writing.]

part in stimulating officials to get any loose rule into sharper shape, and in stimulating lawyers to help them do so. But the case for the convention in its current bold form, begins about here to become materially less persuasive, because the machinery of the convention, however fine in intent, is too loosely adjusted to its purpose. For when the convention is applied to rules which are not in fact available in very guidesome form, those "rules" too are treated as if they *were* guidesome. Sharp guidance must be extracted from their *language*, as if they had been ideally neat and clear. This means that discussion must move in logically slippery sloppy terms; and since the trouble happens exceedingly often in those cases which, having greater elements of doubt, get selected as peculiarly the province of those appellate courts whose writings are recorded,[18] it tends to thrust habits of slippery and sloppy logic into those authoritative writings, and so into the minds and training and habits of thinking of the readers; the profession. That is a price to pay for the convention, if what we want is to outfit ourselves with really well-drawn and effective rules; for nothing so favors either clear drafting of rules or their clear effect as professional habits—not desires, but *habits*—of straight thinking. Where authoritative and therefore "correct" thinking and writing is thus muddy, two things can and do happen. The first is that "rules" which are poor rules because they do not greatly guide are not *seen* and pilloried as poor guides, because they are authoritatively alleged, instead, to have done work which got done by other means; such poor rules thus can and do gain standing, escaping critique and reshaping more often than they are pressed by the convention into new and more useful form. The second thing is that individual leeway left to, and used by, court and other officials escapes notice, and so escapes study—and so leaves us content with a regime of rules less clear than those we need; with a regime of rules most of which are much *less clear than those we have proved by the presence of our best rules that we can produce.*

This brings us to the last point about the lawyers' convention in their professional discourse of treating "the rules" as being the law and all the law, and of treating *phrased* rules as exhausting the subject-matter of "the rules". That point is this, and I do not see it as a net value, though I do view it with a deal of sympathy: the convention contains a majestic machinery

18. [In *The Bramble Bush* (Columbia 1930), Llewellyn emphasized that his claims about the indeterminacy of rules or law were limited to the skewed sample of legal events that constitute the caseload of appellate courts. This phenomenon, now widely discussed under the rubric of the "selection effect," represents a significant qualification of the more extreme Realist claims, and Llewellyn, initially in *The Bramble Bush* and now here, appears to have been the first to recognize it.]

for the perpetuation of itself; it presents every ultimate official action as one which has been dictated by the existing rules; even cases which counsel and the court slip far enough to label openly and officially as "cases of first impression" will be saved from sin by scholars, and decision in such cases will be shown to have been "developed" out of "traditional legal materials" by "traditional techniques". This self-perpetuation of the convention has a number of effects. One is to comfort judges, and to comfort people, when the judges innovate. And, since innovate they must whether they want to or not, and since our official scheme of things is a regimen of divided powers, there is some virtue in that. Another is that the judges are made somewhat slower to innovate; when impending innovation for any reason reaches the stage of consciousness that it will be innovation, the convention and the judges' belief in it contribute to make them hold back. Related is a good portion of blindness in both innovation and in holding back; for so far as "the rules", as they are available in phrased form, are deemed to exhaust the bases for decision, to that extent meditation on other and fruitful things is driven out or driven under cover.

But the last and most directly important effect is that the convention rallies men to resist critique of it and to discourage attempts to correct its defect. The office of rules is to control and guide and unify official behavior. To effect their office they must be clear. To show wherein any rule fails to accomplish that purpose in itself, or wherein other factors than rules play in either to aid or to hamper the guidance and unification of official behavior, or to take one further step toward a more adequate technique of doing the work that rules are for,[19] whether the more adequate technique be by technical improvement of the rules, or by conscious enlistment of other technical tools, or by a more effective combination of both. But the convention, as has been said, gives comfort. To know that we need control of officials, and to believe also that the rules provide it as they stand, is to feel safe. So that if any one attempts to show that the convention is not wholly adequate to represent the facts of legal work, he seems to be attacking the one machinery which can provide the control we need to have. The convention can thus become a fighting faith, and thoughtful scholars can be stung by any challenge to it into taking odd positions—and into attributing to adversaries, real or supposed, positions quite as odd. On the other hand, inquirers seeking fuller understanding, inquirers who find actual control to be less than they supposed, and become bothered by that fact, are capable of preaching

19. [At just this point Patterson wrote "whew!" and suggested that a new sentence might start here.]

their partial insight that the convention is not *wholly* accurate to legal life as if such insight showed the convention to be *wholly* false. Some such extravagances as these have swirled for a decade over the debates about "realism" in jurisprudence.[20] If the controversial writings are reread, each for what it says of positive value, they will be found, despite a touch [of] dialectic exaggeration on each side, to be in rather healthy complement to one another.

This book grows out of that controversy, but will attempt to contribute nothing to it. For the book is centered on the rules of law, which any realistic worker in law must see not only to be existent, but to be highly useful, indeed vital. The approach here is from a technical angle, exploring the ways and meaning of the rules chiefly as part of a legal technician's working material.

The rules of law of course do not make up the whole of our control machinery; for all that there is to law and the things of law is far from making up the whole of our control machinery, and rules of law are far from making up all that there is to law and the things of law. But the rules of law occupy a preferential status. They have a standing and a leverage which gives them peculiar importance. They are also peculiarly open to conscious control, and they are our most familiar agency for conscious control. They are the most mobile and the best mobilizable agency we know. They deserve to occupy a central place. They deserve indeed more sympathetic and flexible study than it is easy to give them if one begins by assuming that they exert, in bloc, the control which, in bloc, they officially purport to.

It is the position of the book that the things which in our legal system pass for rules of law are things exceedingly uneven and variegated. It is the position that the ways in which these variegated rules of law take on meaning and come into operation need combing over with a finer comb than has been their common portion. It is the position that only by sustained and careful attention to how differing types of rule[s] do their work, and how far and where and why the work is or is not effectively done, can we achieve techniques for increasing the effectiveness of our body of legal rules. It is the position that the current conventionalized idealizations about what the rules we have are like, and about how they operate, need severe reexamination because both are so largely false to the facts about rules of law as to get in the way of making effective rules of law. Among other aspects of the

20. [Llewellyn's prickliness about inaccurate caricatures of Legal Realism was longstanding. See Karl Llewellyn, *Some Realism about Realism*, 44 Harv L Rev 1222 (1931).]

matter, the book will urge that, over very considerable areas of law, the accepted ideal of clear rules effectively marking out future official action may itself need serious reexamination; in other words, that some considerable part of the failure of our existing rules to work out according to our current ideology, about how they do work, may be due to a wisdom in our going legal institutions which fits our needs more nearly than does our accepted ideology about those institutions.

For the book rests upon the conception and the belief that while rational thought is vital to effective work in society, and reason is man's distinctive attribute and tool, yet in matters social, reason, if it is to be effective, must be patient. Its span of problem at any given moment is small; its span of immediate attention is small; past solutions must be built into a going social machine, and must be received by new generations which take them as given. Thus, along with error, comes wisdom long built into our going institutions, but received by us not via conscious rational choice but in semi-automatic fashion; and such wisdom often escapes the perception of the later "rational" systematizer of the system of this day. Thus, in the going system of our law, there is much wisdom which seems to have escaped some of the rationalized conventional beliefs about what the system is, and how it goes round, and how it should go round. That going system needs improvement, yes. But the first step most needed in this particular day is a fresh look at the going system itself, and a description which will give us a clearer picture of what it really is and how it really works. From that we may hope to gain light on where there is leverage to improve it, and on what kind of levers to build; we may even gain suggestion about what kind of change may be needed.

My own canvass thus far leads me to believe that there is a great gain in accuracy and in communicability of seeing the going system and the role of the individual within it when, beside the *rule*-stuff, the word-clad and word-limited authoritative formulas, we put on the one hand the body of ideals and idealizations which the lawmen often use without putting or seeing them in words at all, and put on the other hand the institutional patterns, great and small. Which direct perception, which limit and channel imagination, which provide *ways* of doing and thinking and feeling that men "fall into" or "grow into" or "are broken into" as they learn to be and "think like" lawyers. Or, indeed, when they grow into being Americans.

This is the frame of the discussion.

CHAPTER II

Rules of Law: Command and Prediction

We are looking at rules of law from a technical angle. We wish to examine them as devices aimed by people at the controlling of people's behavior. One major controversy among the [scholars of] jurisprudence therefore concerns us only indirectly: the controversy about the "validity" or the "authoritative" nature of a rule "of law" which has no concrete backing by the machinery of the state. There is no desire to belittle the importance of question[s] of rightness or justice in regard to rules; there is no desire to thrust such questions, unconsidered, into a corner. Quite the contrary. But for clarification of terms and of discussion, and in order more effectively to keep in view the problems related to getting ideals for or about legal rules incorporated into rules actually backed by the state-machinery, we shall confine the idea of *rules of law* to such rules as have that backing. For such are the rules with which legal technicians must work, and the rules on which one hopes for increasingly effective work.

There are, however, among the thoughtful men who have been interested in rules of law backed by the state, at least three important lines of emphasis as to the pattern on which to center their discussion of such rules; and each of the three has values. Some see in such rules chiefly *commands*;[1] some see in them chiefly normative propositions laying down that on described facts the proper legal consequence is thus and so;[2] some see in them predictive

1. [The obvious reference here is to John Austin, whose *The Province of Jurisprudence Determined* (Wilfrid E. Rumble, ed, Cambridge 1995) (1832) and *Lectures on Jurisprudence* (Robert Campbell, ed, Cockroft 1875) were staples of English language jurisprudential study from the middle of the nineteenth century until the appearance of H.L.A. Hart's *The Concept of Law* (Clarendon/Oxford) in 1961.]

2. [Here Llewellyn is referring to Hans Kelsen, *Reine Rechtslehre* (1928), later to be translated into English as *Pure Theory of Law* (Max Knight trans, California 1967), but widely known even

propositions giving guidance as to what officials (especially judges) will do, on described facts.[3]

Now in my belief every legal rule for the use of judges is usefully conceived as containing, whatever else it may contain, a command; and the command is addressed to the judges (or other relevant officials), and is a command to do on such facts as the rule describes such things as the rule prescribes. Frequently, but not always, it seems to me useful to see in a rule also a command to relevant laymen; I think it distinctly useful to see in the rules on unlawful homicide not only what their words say, but also and as an inherent part of them a command to people at large not to incur their penalties by committing unlawful homicide. The reasons why I think this way of looking at the matter useful, for technicians doing technicians' work, will appear hereafter. Let it here be taken merely as the expression of a bias.[4]

What is not the expression of a bias, but is the expression of a fact, is that an important part of the work [that] a legal system is *capable* of doing under proper circumstances [is done] by rules which have no touch of precision in the legal consequences which they express or imply. Any command, I suppose, as the word is used, implies that the commander may be displeased at [the] disregard of it, and if displeased may do something about his displeasure; and that much of "legal consequence" lies in the very idea of "command." The point I wish to make is that when anyone insists upon some greater degree of precision in the legal consequence before a "rule" is regarded as attaining the status of a rule "of law", he is idealizing a standard for "rules of law", and limiting the body of rules admitted to that category. And that must be for a reason. The reasons are instructive.

They turn, so far as I can see, on three lines of factor. The first is independent of the size and complexity of the state, but not independent of its political make-up. It is the human drive to want like cases treated alike, which means some degree of trouble and friction if they are not so treated; this urges eternally toward standardization and limitation of consequence

---

in English-speaking countries in the 1920s and 1930s and plainly especially well-known to the German-fluent Llewellyn.]

3. [See Oliver Wendell Holmes, *The Path of the Law*, 10 Harv L Rev 457 (1897).]

4. [This is an intriguing and important paragraph, in which Llewellyn goes from a Kelsen-inspired view of legal rules as commands or empowerments directed to officials to an Austin-inspired view of legal rules as commands to subjects to a Holmes-inspired view of legal rules as predictions of sanctions for noncompliance. But the sentence about homicide is curious. Insofar as legal rules are commands to citizens, they are commands about the primary behavior and not about, or not principally about, sanctions. The state does not appear to be telling us not to incur the penalties that attach to committing homicide; it is telling us not to commit homicide.]

visited, until the very *limitation* can take on at length the status of a right. But it pays to remember, first, that in proper political circumstances the essential likeness among cases may lie exclusively in "displeasing the ruler", or "going counter to command", or "doing what is against the law"; and to remember, second, that it takes time and repetition to crystallize a practice limiting the consequence, and that it takes at least the makings of a practice to crystallize a line of expectation of, say, what it *ought* to mean to "be in mercy" for this rather than for that; and to remember, third, that until a right further crystallizes out of a line of expectation there still is room for policy to shift and for practice to veer off with it. All of which is so easy to see among primitive peoples or in ancient times that we could readily think of it as "not yet law in the modern sense" if we had not yesterday been trying to persuade the traffic cop to let it go with a warning and a promise, or, day before, been reading of a hearing to help the governor determine whether to grant extradition, or been ourselves manoeuvering to keep that Wilkins divorce mess from coming up while Hanrahan was sitting. The ideal, then, that the legal consequence shall be the same for all persons and relevant occasions, and shall be stated and limited with some precision, in the rule of law itself, is an ideal which grows natively out of any regularity which legal proceedings may develop, and which contributes to producing such regularity. It is an ideal which is in this aspect at home when conditions are stable and understood and which is both troubled and troublesome when conditions are novel or in flux or opening new problems. And since law drives always toward regularization, it is an ideal which in this aspect is a very proper *ideal* to have about the perfect form of the rule of law.

The second line of factor urging toward such an ideal for the rule of law has to do with the engineering of a governmental machine, taken purely from the angle of the governors, apart from any interest in the welfare of the governed. The more complex such a machine is, the more difficult to supervise, the greater the number of good men needed, the greater is the appeal of standardization of consequence, along with the appeal of regulation by rule-in-language. Thanks to the first factor mentioned, standardization of consequence can also ease the machine's dealings with the governed. The opposing factor is the well-known need for intelligent discretion on the job when the unexpected happens; but law drives always towards reducing the area of the unexpected, and again the ideal of precise expressed consequence has its point.

The third line of factor is political, and works from the angle of the governed. It expressly envisages the field of needed discretion, and explicitly sacrifices some portion of social utility there, in another interest. The power of governors and officials to be outrageous, arbitrary, tyrannical, biassed in action, is to be limited, even at the cost of limiting their power to be wise, inventive, prophetic solvers of emergent problems.[5] The rule is to define and limit the consequence, that stupid, inexperienced or cowardly officials may be held up, and rash, corrupt or overweening officials be held down. So strong is this phase, of limitation on the powers of officials, in our political philosophy (limitation upwards by cutting power down, limitation downwards by requiring minimum action) that such scholars as [Albert Venn] Dicey and [Roscoe] Pound refer to it as categorically "*the rule of law*", meaning not, any rule, but a *regime* of governing *by* rules of law these very actions of officials which bring the rules of law to bear on others. For our immediate purpose we note in this that the ideal is an of those particular types of political system which stress either rights in the governed or self-limitation in the governors; that is, that it is no necessary part of a concept of "rule of law" in general, unless we are satisfied that only such systems have any business being considered legal systems at all.[6] Secondly, we note again that the ideal, where achieved, comes at a price in effectiveness of good and wise officials. Third, we note that there is room for wide difference of opinion as to the *degree* of precision in defining and limiting legal consequence which is necessary to conform to the ideal—whether, for instance, such a power in a judge as that of indeterminate sentence coupled with a power to suspend sentence may not conflict utterly with the ideal.[7] Lastly, we note that the

5. [An enormous amount of the normative argument in favor of rules is neatly encapsulated in this sentence. Once we realize that rules are prescriptive generalizations that may, as generalizations, produce suboptimal results on particular occasions, we can understand, as Llewellyn plainly did, that limiting discretion by rules in order to limit the unwise use of that discretion comes at the cost of limiting the discretion to be wise and to do good. Conversely, allowing officials the discretion to reach the correct result in particular cases comes at the cost of risking the dangers of the unwise exercise of that discretion. On these themes in the context of rules, see Frederick Schauer, *Playing by the Rules: A Philosophical Examination of Rule-Based Decision-Making in Law and in Life* (Clarendon/Oxford 1991), and in the context of law in general, see Larry Alexander and Emily Sherwin, *The Rule of Rules: Morality, Rules, and the Dilemmas of Law* (Duke 2001); Frederick Schauer, *Thinking Like a Lawyer: A New Introduction to Legal Reasoning* 13–35 (Harvard 2009).]

6. [The view that the only governance systems entitled to be called "law" were those which complied with minimal conditions of generality and limitations on officials was later to be associated most prominently with Lon Fuller, especially in *The Morality of Law* (rev. ed, Yale 1969).]

7. [The conclusion, crisply expressed here, that indeterminate sentencing power may be problematic on rule of law grounds was ultimately embodied decades later in the movement for sentencing guidelines, especially the Federal Sentencing Guidelines, adopted in 1975. The view that such guidelines may impose excess constraint if taken too rigidly was often expressed,

ideal must be an ideal rather than an accurate reflection of what we really have in our legal system, else there would hardly be so much stir about how various rules of law need correction to make them conform to the ideal.

But with these considerations behind us, we can, I think, see why the "mere command" idea is not a useful one for our purposes of inquiry. It is not because a regime of rules consisting of "mere commands" could not under proper circumstances be a very effective ordering of a society, nor is it because commands are no part of the picture of rules of law. It is because when commands are accompanied by an explicitly *limited* consequence, their command aspect loses force and loses importance. By obeying[,] one gets the promised consequence and no more; by disobeying[,] one gets the threatened consequence and no other; the result is to lay out a guide to conduct which looms quite as large in terms of conscious choice as to whether conformity or non-conformity is worth while, *judged by the consequence*, as it can loom in terms of the command. The thinkers who tend toward a predictive approach to rules have seized on, and developed, this truth. But it does not seem to be useful to let the command aspect slide out of sight. We can save its utility and sharpen discussion by leaving it as a part of our conception of a rule of law thus: first, as indicated above, we can treat every rule as containing an appropriate command to any relevant *official*; second, and as to any person affected in his capacity as a directly interested party, we can treat the command or direction element in a rule of law as its *immediate purpose* of channeling behavior, leaving the rest of the rule to be seen as the *technical measure* selected for furthering that purpose. This isolates the technical measure for discussion as such, without divorcing it from the reason of its existence; and so long as we remember that there is no rule unaccompanied in ideal and in fact by some kind of "purpose", we can use the term "rule of law" with some comfort to describe the technical measure.

But we have not by this disposed of the element of soundness and sense which underlies the purely predictive approach to rules of law. The predictive approach starts from the opposite and from the command approach. The latter sets out, so to speak, from the point of view of the personified State dealing with persons subject to that State, and focuses on idealized subjects seen as waiting and willing to obey. The predictive approach sets out, so

and ultimately recognized by the Supreme Court in, for example, *Booker v. United States*, 543 US 220 (2005).]

to speak, from the angle of individuals with no desire to obey anybody,[8] but faced with the fact that there is an outfit known as the State, which sometimes gets in one's way, and sometimes can be harnessed to help one. In either case, on the predictive end, the question is: Then what will the State *do*, and if that cannot be answered, then what will it *probably* do, and what are the limits of error in prediction? Such an approach is quick to break a "rule" down into effective parts, focussing on the legal consequence; but it is quick also to watch for slips and errors in the actual production of the consequence; limits or expenses or delays in procedure loom large; the possibility of crucial witnesses being unavailable are taken account of; not the general rule, but the result in the situation in hand is the focus, and variations among judges or among juries or among other officials, up to and including observation of possible corruption or favor, enter into the picture for estimate. A legal right is calculated and estimated as a prospective market might be calculated and estimated, in terms of what it may be expected to cost to get, and what the getting of it may bring in; and a rule of law acquires significance only in the concrete case in hand.

There are few jurisprudes who have been able to stomach such an ultra-predictive approach to rules of law; there is none whom I have ever read who could use it with consistency; there is too much which it leaves out. But there is no jurisprude whose work is not furthered and sharpened by bearing that approach in mind, and, above all, by testing his own premises and conclusions persistently against the problem of the cynical bad men in repeated concrete situations. For while a rule of law is always more than what it does, yet unless it does a good deal, the more is likely to be a very little more; and it is rare for the heart of its meaning as a technical measure not to be found in what it accomplishes.

The lines of observation which the predictive approach can serve to keep us from forgetting as we labor with rules of law or with any concept of what they are, are such as these: First, that "defined and definite legal consequence", to have meaning, must be a consequence that can be followed clearly and unambiguously to the point of just what official action it involves, at just what cost in time, outlay, or uncertainty. Second, that a "general" rule implies an area and a range of applicability; and that if the area is not clear, neither is the rule; and if there is a *range* of legal effect, the rule falls short of *controlling* official behavior to the exact degree of the range. Third, that the legal consumer (if I may thus English the neat Ger-

8. [Here appears the "bad man," as Holmes designated such a person in *The Path of the Law*, cited in note 3.]

man Rechsinteressent[9]) needs a truly standardized product, not a statistical generalization, and that no rule serves his turn or its alleged purpose unless it is so labelled as to show how far it is to be relied on as a result-producer. All of these points look to the value of neat and accurate verbal formulation of a rule, with an eye especially on just what it applies to, and just what the prescribed legal consequence may be.[10]

But there are other points, related yet distinct, which need a trifle fuller development to bring out at once the contribution of the predictive approach and the reasons why it will not wholly do for our purpose.

The first is that if the prediction approach is carried to its professed conclusion, it becomes an approach which by its nature *can* give no light to an ultimate court on what to do with a hard case. It may guide other officials by telling them what that court will do. It may guide judges in a clear case by telling them the only thing which any intelligent and conscientious judge will do. But the moment the probabilities get at all into balance, the predictive approach forsakes the responsible official looking to the rule of law for guidance and instruction.[11] For this very reason, the ultra-prediction approach has value to the counsellor and the legal consumer; *them* it helps not to mistake the presence of a right rule for an indication that the result will be according to that rule. In reverse, it reminds persons who are formulating rules of law alleged to be *the* rules prevailing in our legal system, that it is the judges whose behavior tests out what rules really prevail. Predictive "rules" are in essence and in themselves not rules of law, they are in essence generalizations about judicial and other official behavior in matters legal.

Yet careful and temperate scholars have insisted that "what the courts will do" is the measure of the rules their study seeks. This leads into the next point, which rests on two peculiarities of our legal system: its centering of thought upon the judge, and its development of much of its law by way of case-to-case decision, in continuous groping generalization, and in heavy reliance on prior decided and recorded cases. In such a system there

9. [Presumably a typographical error, with Llewellyn intending "Rechtsinteressent," the German for a person interested in law.]

10. [Occasionally the part of a rule that designates its scope of application is called the *protasis*, with the part that specifies the consequences that flow from the rule's applicability being labeled the *apodasis*. See Gidon Gottlieb, *The Logic of Choice* (Allen & Unwin 1968).]

11. [In Chapter VII of *The Concept of Law* (Penelope A. Bulloch and Joseph Raz, eds, 2d ed, Clarendon/Oxford 1994), H.L.A. Hart notoriously chides the Realists for ignoring the very point that Llewellyn in fact develops in this paragraph. And in a marginal notation, Patterson notes here that "Cohen" made a similar point about the uses and limitations of a predictive approach in an article in the *University of Pennsylvania Law Review*, presumably referring to Morris Cohen, *On Absolutism in Legal Thought*, 84 U Pa L Rev 681 (1936).]

are always areas of doubt as to just how far the judges meant what they once wrote, or how far new judges will find their meaning wise to follow, or which of three different leads will be the one to be developed. Moreover, particularly in our country with its multitude of jurisdictions, there are doubts as to which judges, on any given point, will win a following among the others; and scholars, as they make their selection and regrouping and rephrasing among the welter of opinions, seeking an order which is always a creation as much as a reflection, enter essentially upon a competition for judicial customers of their views. Not only is deference to the customer a proper selling technique, but most careful diagnosis of the probable market is the key to purveying wares which find a welcome; and, perhaps most of all, in such a system statement *is* prediction, whether that be willed or not; for the rule which will *prevail* tomorrow is today a gamble to foretell. Just as it is good doctrine that judges *ought* to decide tomorrow according to their past decisions—barring statutory change—so also it is blind swallowing of doctrine to overlook the gradual but ceaseless modification in today's decisions of the rules of yesterday. Hence, in the case-law area, there is a juice in a predictive approach which a regime built on official rules set forth in explicit language in statute books finds it hard to comprehend. Hence also American scholars who claim to be searching for accurate statements of what courts will do are not to be read as engaged in mere prediction of judicial behavior. They are engaged in a search for the *rules* of law *which will prevail* tomorrow, when cases come up, and therefore for purposes of guidance *are* the rules today, for layman, for official, and, if the scholar is persuasive, for the judge. This is not the pure prediction of official behavior in the particular case, of the cynic. It is a scholar's careful recognition that with a flurry of competing formulations in the air, each alleged by its proponents to be "the rule of law" for the situation, one who wishes to pick out the *prevailing* rule, the positive rule, the rule which *is* in force with the state-machine behind it, the rule which is the technical device with which we are concerned, will have to observe and perhaps to effectively persuade the judges who are the organs of the state-machine.

By the same token, where the actually prevailing rule *is* clear, in form and in authority, there is no room for this scholar's prediction approach; whether the rule be of statute or of case-law. From this, and from the fact that our most cautious and skilful scholars are likely to profess that approach, one derives a moral. The moral is that our legal woods must be full of rules which are *not* clear.

The last matter which the prediction approach lays close, and lays closest when it is carried to its raw extreme, is that occasional officials can be bought, and more are political hacks or bosses, and the like. Along with the merely human slips of gearing between the official rule and the result, go some slips which are outrage. And right fails, for the man whose remedy is blacked out by dirty play. The vitality in this reminder, for jurisprudence, is to ram home a most uncomfortable dilemma of thought, which no easy juggling of words disposes of. And that dilemma lies in this: that the concepts of *authority*, and of *prevailing*, as applied to *positive* rules of law, are in first instance not concepts of law, but concepts of fact. You test which of two rival governments is *the* government by factual results. You test which of two conflicting state-organs claiming legal authority *has* legal authority in the legal system by which of them maintains its position and throws or jockeys the other out. You test which of the competing alleged rules of law is *the* positive rule of law by which one gains factual acceptance by the highest courts.[12] At this point, and suddenly (and with reason!) you stop the testing by pure resultant and effective fact, and begin the testing of the facts of official behavior, including the behavior of judges on highest tribunals, by some standard (say "rules of law") derived from something else than that behavior.

The break in thought is clear; what is its reason? Its reason is that the ultra-predictive approach to rules of law makes clear as no other intellectual device can, because the ultra-predictive approach gets down to even the most irritating facts of concrete life. That is, that the purely positive basis of official *behavior* is not in itself regular enough to afford an adequate indication of what rules are in force. Repeatedly, it *is* regular enough. Often, it is not. The first escape from this, while still resting on fact and effectiveness as a test of what rules *have* state-sanction, is to pick out particular, limited, bodies of officials as *the* authoritative organs to be watched. So, in our system, [with respect to] Constitution-making bodies, and statute-making bodies (whose pronouncements are laid down in formal official words) and ultimate courts (whose pronouncements are laid down in their judgments and more informal exposition of their reasoning), what I [now] wish to urge is not only (as will be developed later) that this does not escape

12. The foregoing sentences remarkably anticipate Hart's idea of the *ultimate rule of recognition*, developed at length in *The Concept of Law*. The extent to which to which these ideas, whether in Hart or in Llewellyn, were inspired by Kelsen's less factual (and more of a transcendental understanding) notion of the *Grundnorm* could be the source of intriguing speculation. And for the real world application of Llewellyn's conjecture about rival governments and competing sources of ultimate legal authority, see F.M. Brookfield, *The Courts, Kelsen, and the Rhodesian Revolution*, 19 U Tor L J 326 (1969); J.W. Harris, *When and Why Does the Grundnorm Change?*, 29 Camb L J 117 (1971).]

the dilemma, but more important, and immediately, that to take refuge in such isolation of particular authoritative organs, *if one rests content therewith,* is to turn the conceptions of "prevailing", "positive", "backed by the State", into fictions untested and misleading, and to allow the attention to be diverted from the essential tasks of law, and of rules of law. For the office of law in the aspects we are discussing is not to lay down standards, merely, for the measuring of behavior and the possible detection of undesired variants; nor is it, merely, to clothe in words rules which persons of position announce as being the rules "of the State". The office of law in these aspects is *to control official behavior and to channel it.* And for rules of law to *prevail,* for them to *be,* as *positive* rules, they require to be sufficiently observed or followed in action *so that they count in the behavior* of the State machine.

Now the only thing which stands in the way of moderately effective reconciliation of this obviousness with the policy and practice of current thinking about what rules prevail is our habit of answering the question of whether a given rule "is law" with a Yes or a No. It is the fashion of legal discourse to assume that a particular rule under discussion either *is* "the law of the State" or is *not,* and that there is no middle ground. Yet we have the intellectual wherewithal to talk and think more sanely. It is not alone that we know of "conflict of authority" within these United States, on common law points. We also find counsellors who tell us that such and such is the rule in the First Department, but the Fourth Department seems unlikely to accept it. We find administrators following "the interpretation of this office", and lawyers dealing with them. We have, in a word, a modus vivendi, and a modus dicendi, and a modus intelligendi, for dealing with what may be long-time intervals during which the ultimate oracle on what rule prevails may go unheard. We have more. We have instances a-plenty in which it is not the rule, but is lines of action supposedly controlled by a single unchanged rule or set of rules which do the varying. There is "the practice of the office"; there is the known propensity of one judge to deal technically with procedural points; there is the building up of a line of business practice and understanding, with settlement of anything that looks like a test case until the chosen line of practice can hope to be too firmly settled to disturbed; there are regional or temporal variations in policy of enforcement. There are rules which are never challenged or applied in court because they are so well understood and lived by, and rules which are not lived by at all, but which go over long periods unapplied in court because the persons who would benefit by application are ignorant or helpless. And it is within the sphere of such varying *partial,* more-or-less *prevalence* of rules-backed-by-

"the-State" that most legal work of the profession is carried on. This is no situation for jurisprudence to ignore, fixing its attention upon a Yes or No answer to whether a rule "is law".

What we have in the broad range of the "positive", as the predictive approach has helped us see, is first, the *rules of ultimate authority*, partly known, and partly only to be reached by prediction. We can agree that these are the standards for judging all others; such is our positive and prevailing system. But part of that system is also that many of the ones most important to some-of-us go long unknowable. Some pine away, their death made fully known only by an inquest in some later test-case. Meantime, backed by *pieces* of "the State", there are many other rules which are *partially* "of law" to the extent that they do positively prevail, by region, by span of time, by department of government, by line of trade or other economic activity, by personality of official. They are too unstable to make a systematizer of "the rules of law" feel comfortable, and his groans are heard when too many, say, of lower court decisions, are forced upon his attention by law publishers' initiative. But they are as they are, and lawyers have to live with them.

Such a situation is hard neither to see nor to state; it is a simple recognition of the simple fact that neither "the State" or "prevalence" is more of a unit than it is, even while each remains as much of a unit as it is. The difficulty may seem a bit increased when we come to action *or general rulings* by officials which are at odds, either, first and in substance, with the clear ultimate rules; or second, and in motivation, with our rules and our vaguer but still definite understanding about what should motivate officials; or third, and in technique, with our notions and rules about handling like cases alike. But I find here no real difficulty. Let any official action be seen for what it is in its effect: a bid, intentional or unintentional, toward the making of a rule of law out of like action, a bid, tentative or forceful, for self-legitimation by ultimate creation of a rule of ultimate authority to give it standing. The line of measurement becomes clear at once, the line of legitimacy or illegitimacy, the sphere of doubt, the procedure for testing, or correction, or castigation—or of accolade. To generalize the action into the form of rule is to give it its intellectual testing-frame. To set it against the rules of ultimate authority is to judge it. To find doubt is to move toward clarification.

But to disregard the actions, though they be a discrepant welter, of the multitude of state officials who are not "the legislature" and "the ultimate court" is to duck away from the most pungent point of the concept "backed by the State", and from following rules "of law" through into *performance* of their office. For without effectiveness, a rule is paper only, not backed by, nor sanctioned by the State, but mouthed or printed merely, and left unprevailing. *A rule cannot prevail in any State save to the extent that it cogs into that State's going institutional structure.*

Thus from the command approach to rules of law we derive utility on the side of purpose; from the predictive approach we derive utility on the side of effective meaning and indeed existence as a positive rule, and a concept of partial, limited prevalence, to be contrasted with an ultimate prevalence, and with the ideal situation in which ultimate prevalence is accompanied by uniform effect on all official action. But between these approaches, and necessary to give body to either of them in their application to work with rules of law, lies the *technical* measure itself: that frame of thought and words we call "a rule". And the type of frame of thought and words involved in the technical measure raises problems of its own.

CHAPTER III

Rules of Law: The Propositional Form

Preface to Rules III[1]

There seem to be at least three lines of problem which trouble every grouping of men, and which summon and organize activity, men, and machinery for their solution. One is the disposition of felt grievance and of the disputes commonly attendant on felt grievance. One is the channeling of conduct and expectation in areas fraught with possible conflict and tension, in such manner as to hold down the tension, to hold off or eliminate conflict, and, positively, to further coordination of activities toward end of group-import. A third is fixing up machinery to determine whose say is to be *the* say when some novel problem needs solution, and for getting that say duly said and known.

In our Great Society, an important portion of the handling of these problems has been taken over by what we call The State, and The State works and speaks largely in the persons of officials in office, and one of the important devices used by the officials and approved by the rest of us consists of what we know as rules of law. And one essential characteristic of our own Great Society and of our State along with it is that we conceive such rules of law to properly guide and control the conduct not only of the rest of us, but also of the officials.

It is, however, obvious that the jobs mentioned at the outset as needing to be done do actually get done, so far as they do get done, by the actions of people, including especially people who are officials in office. And it is

1. [The title "Preface to Rules III" is Llewellyn's, but it is not clear whether Llewellyn intended this as a chapter preface, or whether it was originally a preface to the entire book, or whether it was written as a preface to a shorter work but then tentatively moved to the beginning of Chapter III.]

obvious that people doing those jobs, like people doing any other kind of job which is both difficult and recurrent, will have worked out for the purpose recognizable lines of activity and skill which we know as crafts. And the presence of various legal crafts among us is a fact. We have them. They are in use. We can recognize among others a craft of judging, with at least two major subdivisions, that of judging in first instance, at first official presentation of the facts, and that of judging in review. We can recognize a craft of advocacy, a craft of counselling, a craft of teaching prospective lawyers, a craft of legislating, a slue of crafts of administering government. It does not require deep thought to perceive that our rules of law without these crafts would not do, or indeed mean, or indeed be, what they now are. And it is a fair hypothesis that a jurisprudence might be fruitful which focussed not on "Law" as its essential subject-matter, but on the jobs which Law is there to help get done; a jurisprudence which therefore viewed the crafts as a major tool for doing the jobs, and viewed Rules of Law in turn not as its sole subject-matter, but rather as a major tool for the use of the crafts, and for partial control of the craftsmen.

Such a jurisprudence would not, in concern over the crafts and the Rules of Law, forget the craftsmen who "carry" the craft into action and from generation to generation—nor indeed the books which record the craft's experience and its theorizing. And of the craftsmen it would have to remember that they are *both* men *and* craftsmen. In both capacities it would be strange if they did not now display a fine idealism, and, again, forget it. In both it would be strange if they did not, today, shape a shrewd tool, and tomorrow a clumsy one, and rest content with both. Indeed, when there are so many of them, it would be strange if their craft showed sharply standardized coherence and uniformity, whether of tradition, performance, or character.

Such a jurisprudence, then, would face the miracle of how we could have the elbows of one hundred and thirty million people somehow kept sufficiently out of one another's ribs and faces to get along, and of how we could get some degree of similarity of judgment out of more than a hundred and thirty thousand of men of law—it would face that miracle not as a given and an of-courseness, but as a strange thing under the sun whose marvelous ways deserved to be explored with awe and trepidation. The miracle is far enough from full perfection in its functioning to allow of no doubt that we need to tinker with it somehow. We do tinker. We must. Yet to tinker without understanding is dangerous work. And mere acceptance is a poor help to understanding.

This book is an essay at seeing our Rules of Law in such a setting, as technical measures for getting things done that need doing; as technical measures in the hands of craftsmen who are people, the men of law; as technical measures played upon by ideal and purpose at the one end, played upon and playing upon, at the other, the institutions of the craft and of the Great Society. It is an essay in philosophy of law, if "philosophy" be taken in its older sense as including any effort to discover how this or that goes round and what it means; and if "law" be taken as including any study of the jobs law is there to help do, and of our human ways of getting these jobs done. Or it could be regarded as a pre-scientific essay in sociology, if sociology includes putting side by side pieces of ancient common sense about crafts and rules and words and people, and trying to make a more ordered sense out of seeing them side by side instead of scattered. Or, on the technical side, it could be regarded as stump-pulling for a theory of rules of law in the American legal system and for a theory also of dogmatics. But how to classify the essay seems to me of relatively little moment if it can only succeed in making somewhat clearer the problems of guidance and control by our rules of law, toward our ideals, and through our craftsmen.

Rules of Law: The Propositional Form

As we have seen, to envisage rules of law merely as commands is to leave out of the picture what for the lawyer is their very life-blood: the indication of what he or anyone else can do or can be expected to do about any given situation; and it is to leave the state official either without authority to proceed in the event of breach, or vested with boundless discretion. So firmly rooted is our tradition that judges, for instance, have no business to be left thus that judges themselves have invented a damning legal classification for mere commands, a classification which comes very close indeed to meaning "nugatory in court."[2] More commonly than not, judges speak of such mere commands as "only directory," and mean thereby that so far as the judges are concerned, other people are free to disregard the legislative language if they choose to. Thus if an Eighteenth Amendment[3] wishes to assure itself of teeth which cog with the institutional machine of the State, and which set that machine in motion, its own merely prohibitory language

2. [Llewellyn shifts in Chapter III to more frequently placing his punctuation marks inside the quotation marks rather than, as in Chapters I and II, to placing them outside. Although this is of no significance in itself, it does suggest a substantial passage of time between the completion of Chapter II and the commencement of Chapter III.]

3. [This is the constitutional amendment adopting Prohibition.]

must be "implemented" by something like the Volstead Act.[4] The *normality*, in a statistical sense, of finding a purported rule of law accompanied by its prescribed and definite legal consequence is in other words so outstanding that lawyers and the law officials themselves feel the command that lacks fixed consequence for breach to be technically deficient not only in form but in substance as well. On the other hand, if the command be seen as the essence, but the prescription of legal consequence still viewed as a necessary part of the rule, the result is esthetically painful. For it grates to be dealing with commands which devote half of their language and of their effort and of their effect to envisaging disobedience and taking care for it. Thus, the "anomaly" about a rule of law, that it "is made for the purpose of covering its own breach" is an "anomaly" which depends on first seeing the rule as in fundamental sense a command; and it is a fair criticism that a way of looking at a rule's essence which forces the immediate setting up in the picture of an anomaly which goes to the heart of form and function is an unpromising intellectual approach.

On the other hand, as we recall, a purely predictive phrasing of a relation between fact situation and legal consequence gives guidance to a counsellor which it does not give to a court of last resort. Moreover, it strains the imagination to conceive of legislators intent on changing a rule of law because they do not like it drawing their statute with an eye to prediction alone. Prediction a legislature must do if it is to legislative effectively; of which more hereafter. But the rule it shapes has a purpose and function of control that uses prediction-stuff only as its raw material.

Perhaps the greatest difficulty with a purely predictive approach, however, is intellectual. No intellectual tool or construct is useful where it is unmanageable; and a purely predictive approach will, for a long time to come, find too many areas of law in which knowledge fails it. To begin with, this is because a general predictive statement has too wide a range of official personnel, to take account of, and too wide a range of case, too wide a range of possible advocates who may be handling different cases. Indeed, it is the narrowing of the field of study along any or each of these dimensions which puts the counselling lawyer into position to do usably accurate prediction. Again, even where knowledge suffices, the approximately accurate statement of a general predictive proposition requires such a profusion

4. [The Volstead Act did indeed, as Llewellyn says, implement in statutory form the Eighteenth Amendment's prohibition on the sale of alcoholic beverages, but the example is epiphenomenal. Most constitutional provisions impose directly enforceable obligations on the states or federal government or both, and do not need supplementary statutes to ensure their effectiveness.]

of qualification as to embarrass use of the statement when achieved. And partly for this reason, partly because language is conventional and rules of law are not by the body of our lawyers or of our people conceived as either being pure predictions or as meant to be, partly because formulas implying the most inaccurate of predictions are in current use among our law folk as *being* rules of law—for such reasons as these, accurate predictive generalizations are not reasonably *communicable* "as rules" even among the law folk, within the framework of their going institutions. Now it is not sense to deal with anything as constituting the rules of, and for, an institution which the men of the institution do not or cannot or will not understand as being or communicating their rules.

This brings us back to a "rule of law" as a general proposition indicating a general situation of fact and prescribing for any concrete situation falling within the class a legal consequence of described and limited character. Most lawmen would agree that such is, roughly, the characteristic form of the technical rule of law as they see it and deal with it in the trade. As we shall see, it may be questioned whether such agreement would rest on solid observation; but what does rest on solid observation is this: if a form of words of the character just described turns up, any lawman will at once recognize it as purporting to be a rule of law. That is more than can be said for either mere commands or accurate predictions.

There are, however, tricks to the trade of jurisprudence. And while most such tricks serve legitimate and useful purposes (such as here, providing a characterization of a "rule of law" which is both usable, recognizable by the profession, and an excellent focus of study) yet the tricks need to be put into slow motion in order that we may not lose sight of the disappearing difficulties, and so that we may not conceive them to be gone if they happen to be only covered up.

Take first this matter of prescription of legal consequence. That idea and its formula have [] power which does not appear on the simple-seeming surface. The elements and effects packed into them need examination in order that we may maintain our orientation. For by the phrasing "prescription of legal consequence," at one stroke and as if with a *single* solvent idea, the "command" aspect of a rule is both satisfied, and masked, and limited. Somebody (the sovereign) or some body (the State) lays down what consequence *is to* follow on a given type of fact-situation; this is done with authority (by a superior to an inferior); "legal consequence" instructs and orders the judge, even though it does not explicitly mention either him or the order, and it promises or threatens to everybody else an instructed[,] and a limited, judge; the prescription is "positive," because there are indeed judges, and they have the state-machine behind them, and there is real likelihood that they will in their actions take due note of the prescription. (By the same token, as will hereafter be developed at length, the "purpose" phase of the command also enters into the formulation as an inherent aspect of the technical determination of its meaning.) At the same stroke any difficulties of prediction are sidestepped by the formula; they are swept not away, but under the bed. For it can be pointed out that the consequence is not "foretold," but prescribed; the defendant who cannot be found, the dead or perjured witness, the prejudiced jury, the blundering lawyer, the perverse court, the vanishing assets, these thus slide away from attention as being consequences *not* "prescribed." And the "legal" part of the "legal consequence" can in any situation which might threaten embarrassment be phrased broadly enough or loosely enough to throw all such matters into the implicit twilight of "procedure," or of slips in procedure. Lastly, the formula moves the rule into the realm of Oughtness; the rules becomes a "precept," or a "norm," that Ought to be followed. (Note: on the ambiguity here anent "rule of conduct" see Ch. V.) This frees it, in simple seeming, from the necessity of being checked up by factual results (which simply Ought to conform to it). This also masks from view the inescapable problem of factual effect which lies in the attribute of "positivity" or "prevailingness." So far as I can make out, there is here a real threat and barrier to clear thinking; for it seems to be hard for a jurisprude who thinks in these terms to focus at the same time on the Ought-character of the legal consequence and on the factual presuppositions of there being any positive character in the rule—a difficulty which we sought in the last chapter to cut away by recognizing that positivity could be and commonly was a question less of Yes or No than of extent, of intensiveness, and, generally, of degree.[5]

A further effect of this removal of the rule to the realm of Oughtness also needs mention. A *command* is flavored with an ideal element of *purpose*. But it is very easy to see the commander, and to disapprove of his purpose. The conception of a positive rule of law as a command invites [the] contrast of positive rules with just rules, with right rules, with ethically valid rules. Such a contrast is valuable, but it is also extremely uncomfortable if it lies so close

5. [Most contemporary versions of legal positivism incorporate what H.L.A. Hart in *The Concept of Law* (Penelope A. Bulloch and Joseph Raz, eds, 2d ed, Clarendon/Oxford 1994) called a "rule of recognition," the rule that specifies whether some other rule is or is not a valid rule of law. Llewellyn's suggestion here and in the previous chapter that legal validity might be a matter of degree is an intriguing variant on, or challenge to, the standard positivist "yes or no" account of legal validity and the operations of rules of recognition, but this is not the place to explore fully whether Llewellyn's challenge is, in the final analysis, successful.]

as to occur too easily or too often; moreover, if it occurs too often, the contrast loses weight. He who is not moderately anchored in the legal system of his time and place may be a prophet, but his honor will commonly be slow in coming to him; a Blackstone found a market which a Bentham lacked.[6] It is then worth note that Oughtness "of legal consequence" has an appeal which positive command does not. It is flavored not with the tyranny of Caesar—to whom after all we have been enjoined to render only that which is Caesar's—but with the majesty of the System of The Law, in favor of which right-minded men have from the beginning resolved all doubts. We have seen in our inquiry into the peculiar osmotic relation of Is and Ought and Will Be in American case-law that questions of *positivity* of a rule of law lie in a borderland of flux between the three.[7] We add here that the Oughtness of a legal consequence in a propositional form of rule lies in an inevitable and similar flux between *legal* rightness and *ethical* rightness. The rule of law has as one of its functions to be right and just. Ethics in thought, language and emotion are close, and osmosis will not down.

Again I wish to avoid misconception. I am *not* saying merely that the natural law and natural right line of thinking, or any line of thinking which sees "justice" or "rightness" as a proper element in any proper rule of law, is an instrument for shaping and reshaping positive law. I am *not* saying that such shaping and reshaping does not commonly proceed by a fallacy of ambiguous middle which needs to be made clear and can be made clear by a legal craftsman conscious of his techniques. The line of the argument under such reshaping runs roughly: "Where there is a [positive legal] right there is a positive legal remedy. Here there is a [natural, ethical] right. Ergo . . ." Which is exposable fallacy. What I am saying is that the reason why such an easy fallacy is palatable and is employed rather than exposed and cast out is not only because men desire to see the rules of law be just and right in perception and in effect, but because they believe in general the rules *are* so; with the result that to show the line of justice is per se to make case for having shown the line of the positive rule *in any point of doubt*. It is, further, that beside any particular ethical or natural value to be served by a rule and to be weighed in shaping it there sit two other values of both ethics and of

6. [On the intriguing notion that legal ideas have markets, Llewellyn's observations have a contemporary counterpart in Jamal Greene, *Selling Originalism*, 97 Geo LJ 657 (2009)

7. [In referring to these relations as "osmotic," Llewellyn appears to be suggesting some degree of back and forth or interpenetration in both directions.]

natural law,[8] which call no less for weighing: the value of abiding by the legal system as a whole, and the value of protecting expectations fairly based upon its any detailed part. It is, finally, that the Ought flavor of the "prescription of legal consequence," whether or not designed to avoid contact with distasteful irregularity in actual effects, carries the rule inescapably into a realm in which these factors of osmotic flux operate between desired ideal and existing law. It carries the rule there, and it should, just as it should include the necessary factual-effect problem raised by the prediction-thinkers, and should include the necessary purpose and direction problems raised by the command-thinkers. But, and this is the value of the showing in slow motion, this flux into ethics is not revealed on the verbal *surface* of the proposition expressing the "positive rule of law."

With jurisprudential and verbal shells now removed from these valuable and elusive peas, so that we can bear in mind both that they *are* on the table and their relation to one another, the propositional concept of a positive rule of law is freed of troubles in its uses. And it at once shows its true character as the most valuable and useful concept of a rule which has yet been invented.

It is valuable first because it fits smoothly into the going speech-usage of the profession. As has been indicated, any lawyer dealing with any problem is looking for a rule of law to cover it, and any lawyer recognizes as a rule (allegedly or actually positive) a formula setting forth in general terms a type of fact-situation and laying down a legal consequence therefor. The concept fits not only the speech-usage but the working practices of the profession. In novel cases, where elliptical statement would be ambiguous, this is the most convenient form for a rule to have, so that statutes mostly are and certainly ought to be built after this pattern. Case-law rules, too, gain clarity and precision as they are thrown into it.

The pattern is practically valuable also in easing argument, focussing issues, furthering clarification of the implications of a rule; or if the formula concerned by an alleged rule, or a candidate for ruleship, then in furthering critique of it by making clear what it would contain and portend if it should be adopted. For the pattern is a pattern whose use and manipulation have long been the study of logicians. Closely related are other virtues worth listing separately: the propositional pattern of a rule, by its very invitation to clarify implication, invites as a consequence precision of its own language;

8. [In referring to "natural law," Llewellyn is plainly referring only to the reality or objectivity of morality, and not to any form of natural law, whether from Aquinas or anyone else in the natural law tradition, as a theory of law.]

and that precision is invited not only in the term containing the sphere of application—the description of the type-fact-situation—but also in the term containing the legal consequence. And a large measure of precision is a goal not only technically, so as to expose to lawman and perhaps to layman, early, what the rule means; but it is also an interstitial goal along the road to critique of the rule in its aspect as a measure, for precision makes clear, early, the *limitations* resting on the rule when viewed as a means.

Equally, then, to commander, to lawyer-technician, to jurist or philosopher, to predicter, to administrator and to judge, the propositional form and concept of a rule of law is useful, doubly useful because its concept is so adjusted to its material and the uses thereof as to press constantly toward the turning of loose or vague "rules" into more effective actual technical devices. And it is trebly useful because the quantum of command, of purpose, of prediction, and of ethics which it implicitly includes is, like the quantum of legal consequence which it expressly includes, neither loose nor large, but limited and shaped by and to the going ways of the legal system concerned. So much of these elements as are in the legal system as that system works, as it changes by its own internal processes: that is the included quantum. So much leeway for those elements as the system actually gives, in the play of its gears and the adjustment of its labor to the life within and around it: that is the leeway which is implicit. This in no way impairs the rule of law as a measure having body and shape and limits, as a technical device within a going scheme, with which one can compare and perhaps contrast purpose in general, or perfection of effectiveness, or ethical virtue. For just as the express legal consequence in the proposition itself is not only indicated but also limited, so also with the quantum of the other elements which are implicit in it. By their presence, they give to the rule meaning as a working part of a going scheme: *positive* indeed. But by the positive limitation on their degree of presence, as that limitation is *given* by the going legal *scheme of things*, they leave open for comparison and contrast any larger or looser or other aspect of purpose, or of justice or ethical virtue, or of predictability or regularity or bias of actual incidence.

Again, the utility is obvious, equally to commander, to lawyer-technician, to jurist or philosopher, to predicter, to administrator and to judge. To each the propositional form of rule offers a technical measure for his consideration which is just to his demands, in that it includes within the positive rule of law so much of the element he is most interested in as has in the going legal system a positive basis for inclusion; and it offers each a technical measure which is just to his need, in that it offers, for comparison and for use, a something with body and limits to work with or to work on, a something firm enough to contrast with either ideal or actuality, with either purpose or effect. And the rule of positive law in propositional form, thus offered, has the final value that it can, as a technical center and meeting-ground, be the same for all, whatever their interests or spheres of action. Plainly, it is the concept of "rule of law" needed for this book.

Now it will be observed that the concept of rule of law which we have been discussing has in the process of discussion acquired a number of attributes over and above its general propositional form, over and above its indication of some type of fact situation, and [over and above] its prescription of a legal consequence both indicated and limited. It has acquired certain attributes familiar in the literature, but it has acquire[d] them with a touch and twist individuated to our purposes, and that individuation requires to be made explicit.

Not formal in character, but having to do with the real or assumed organ of formulation, is the attribute of *authority* in the rule. We are not at the moment concerned with historical genesis, but with dogmatic status, in this regard. It matters not at the moment who gave a given rule its authority or its form; what matters is that all rules we shall discuss will be discussed either as being rules that have authority or as being rules appropriate to have authority; and they will be discussed in the context of their possibly having or acquiring that status: rules conceived as *for* legislative enactment, or as *for* acceptance by the highest courts. On the case-law side of our literature most of our familiar rules are of this type. They are formulated *for* acceptance and use by future judicial action; and it is not our habit to distinguish purely hypothetical rules as being hypothetical unless we conceive it as verging on the hopeless to persuade courts that what prior courts have done really fits the pattern we propose for future acceptance. On the legislative side, on the other hand, the practice of fixed formulation thrusts discussion into "meaning" and "construction" of a frame of words already taken as inescapably providing "the rule." The difference in our lines of attack there and in case-law brings home to us that where language is fixed, leeway is lessened. This joins with our convention that judges are to follow the past, while legislators are free to lay down frank and far reaching change[s] in a rule, to make more frequent in discussion of legislation the explicit distinction the Europeans love between *de lege lata* and *de lege ferenda*.[9] But both rules

9. [This is the familiar distinction between what the law is and what the law should be.]

"made" and rules "to be made" are discussed on the assumed premise of authority in them.

Related, but with a different emphasis, is the assumption of *positivity* in the rules we shall discuss. An *authoritative* rule is in one sense by the fact of being authoritative a positive rule within the purview of the authority concerned. We shall, however, find it worth while to distinguish. It is convenient to take authority on the side of recognition of the rule's *claim* to observance; it is convenient to take positivity on the side of the degree, kind, and extent of actual observance which man can perceive in the world of fact. There is a touch of weaseling in this proposed division, in that *recognition* is itself a concept of fact; but the weasel is one capable of muzzling, with care; and we do need language to describe the situation where "true" authority lies still in doubt, but partial positivity is at work, or where true authority is recognized but is also disregarded in a quiet practice which may in due course either undermine the authority or, as the case may be, jail the disregarders. At any rate, rules herein discussed will be discussed also on the basis of their having actually or hypothetically positive character in this sense of being going rules in a going legal scheme, with some portion of the going force of a going State-machine behind them.

This implies an attribute in our rule of law which is less conventionally familiar. It is not a formal attribute, but a functional one. The rule conceived as geared into a going legal scheme operated by the existing personnel of that going legal scheme is conceived also and of necessity as having the meaning of its language determined in terms of the ways and the thought-patterns of the men of the relevant legal system. This is so obvious that unless it is made explicit we might overlook or forget it; it is indeed too obvious to have received properly sustained attention. And we shall not be safe if we overlook or forget it; for it is here that the full range of implication lies, implication of references, of flux, of leeway, of limitation by practice and context, some portions of which were considered earlier in this chapter. These implications are part of the *positive meaning* of any rule of law. They always narrow and limit its possible meaning; they frequently distort its meaning from its framer's purpose; they sometimes supply its meaning. Their presence is one major reason for centering this book upon our own legal system and its rules, so that there may be at least a roughly homogeneous background of implicit reference.

Side by side with this functional attribute sits another: rules of law are rules with the function of accomplishing control by language-communication. There are two elements in this: language-communication, and accomplishment of control. I think also that one must include at least one particular type of control, and that is: to get significantly similar matters of raw emergent fact handled in significantly similar fashion by officials, irrespective of the differing intelligence, personality, interests and background of the officials. I have no illusion that this is accomplished by rules of law as such and in general; but I do think that a significant degree of its accomplishment is an almost universal ideal for rules of law, and I think further that no alleged rule which does not in some measure move in action toward such a rule can widely be regarded as a *positive* rule at all. Now to move toward such a result by way of language-communication requires that the *language* indicate clearly enough what raw emergent fact is covered by the rule so that there *can* be drawn from *the* language by reasonable technicians significantly similar lines of guidance about what fact situations do, and what fact situations do not[,] fall within the rule. If the rule's language, *in the context of the legal system*, does not admit of this, then the "rule," however thoroughly accepted as such, fails of a necessary functional attribute. It becomes not a rule, but a pseudo-rule of law.

At this point the state of recent literature makes it needful to insert a word which in a non-controversial context would be needless. What I have just written *says* that unless the language of a purported rule of law is clear enough to mean roughly similar things to different officials about what to do with raw emergent states of fact, that purported rule fails to perform the office of a rule of law; it fails to the extent to which its meaning varies. That I wrote such an observation implies two things. It implies first that I do not like such a situation of failure in office by a rule. It implies secondly that I think the failure, in our legal system, frequent enough and bad enough to need study and worry. It does *not* imply that I do not know that there are in our system many admirably drawn and sweetly effective rules of law, nor does it imply that I am judging those rules by the others and denying the existence or importance of the good ones. It implies on the contrary that I am judging the bad ones by the good ones, seeing their defects against the pattern of what we can do, as proved by the welcome fact that we have sometimes done it, and done it not by guess but by plan. The contrast between our technically good and our technically poor rules cannot be fobbed off by any flummery of explaining how good the good ones are. And that our best ones are *not* the general run is simple to demonstrate. First, if they were, it would verge on the criminal to give so large a portion of our law curricula over to study of how to deal with not-so-clear rules.[10] Second, no lawyer with *any* case that falls outside the established run of his own experience feels safe until he has tested any rules he finds in books against an arduous exploration of his own; and he feels safer if he can get the opinion of a man experienced in the field of the case, *and* an able one, whose *judgment* he trusts. The not-so-clear rules are plentiful enough to beguile the teaching profession and the practitioners into wrestling long and hard with the problems which their frequency is thought to raise. A jurisprude has then no call to apologize for giving to the same problem a due mead of attention. Indeed one can cite on the question a saying not unfamiliar in courts of last resort, whose very familiarity both buttresses the point and helps explain why making it is necessary: "Had it not been for the remarkable diversity of opinion among the judges who have participated in this case, I should myself have thought the matter too plain for argument."

Before leaving the point of effecting control, it may be worth passing notice that even a rule whose language is plain to the willing eye may be drawn to a purpose at which the eye rebels. So that this aspect of accomplishing control with some urge toward significant similarity of result may even lap over into including a requirement that the rule's very purpose be at least not so obnoxious to too many of the relevant officials that it can count on being deliberately twisted out of intended meaning.

At the minimum, in any event, the control aspect requires *some* degree of clarity of language in the rule, on the side of when it does and when it does not apply, and of course some similar degree as to the legal consequence of its application. This at once suggests maximum clarity and precision as an attribute of the optimum ideal type of rule of law.

And we cannot do without discussion of an ideal optimum type. In the first place, the very propositional form of [a] rule of law is itself an ideal type, not a description of the actual and current rules. Current rules may be in that form or they may not. Current rules are very commonly elliptical in phrasing; on the case-law side, they rarely have an accepted form of precise wording—what is "the universally accepted rule" is an *idea*, not a phrasing; and its content varies on its edges and in its direction and emphasis accord-

10. [Perhaps not in Llewellyn's day, but several generations of law students and lawyers have since then complained that the law schools' overwhelming focus on hard appellate cases is unfaithful to the reality of a legal world dominated by easy cases and clear rules.]

ing to how one gets around to reducing it (or expand[ing] it) into words. Elliptical formulation opens leeway for material variation in the filling in of the ellipsis; it will not do to speak lightly of fitting it into the propositional pattern, nor will it do to observe merely that any elliptical phrasing can of course be cast into the "fuller and more accurate" form; for what is current and positive is the shorthand *with its leeways and its inexactness*. Any one (or more) of the *possible* more exact propositions which it suggests and squares with but does not determine is thus an ideal form of rule which we set up to better see, describe and measure the "rule" which *is* current.

Into the use of some ideal type, for better canvass, description and critique we are thus obliged to go: needs must, when the existing phenomena to be discussed are of no single type. While we are at it, I think it worth while to reach for a more narrowly formulated ideal optimum type, as a more accurate tool for description and evaluation. For on two matters our propositional form runs thus far wholly unbounded: it must be "general"—but how general? It must be precise of application, to give guidance—but how precise? I can answer neither question, but I think I see the lines of an approach, and a way of describing an optimum ideal rule which can be used to sharpen our discussion.

CHAPTER IV

Rule of Thumb and Principle

Precision of legal rule, maximum precision, utter precision, has danced like a will o' the wisp before legal thinkers as an ideal to be attained, or if not attained, then approached. The precision desired has aimed at two goals now familiar to us: guidance, and limitation. But, and this we shall do well to bear in mind, the legal thinkers have done their aiming very largely with, and against the background of, an ancient ideology, the ideology of formal logic conceived as a discipline not merely descriptive of the relations of classes and propositions, but descriptive also of the existing world. Now it happens that no man has yet been able to build categories to neatly and significantly box the multiple conflicts and relations with which men of law must deal; so that logical precision of a legal structure, in the sense of formal logic, is a precision which would squeeze intolerably. But it happens also that law is a highly practical institution, and that lawmen manage, one way or another, to square their activities measurably with the life around them, no matter what ideology they may be using; lawmen will not be faithful to an ideology which will not do their work. Still, if the dominant ideology is faulty as a tool for coping with life, then law and people suffer; they suffer to the degree that the lawmen's practical and implicit corrections are delayed or are inadequate. As the reader is by now aware, the writer is of [the] opinion that the richest ore of a corrected ideology is found in location and study of the corrective devices the lawmen have invented to make the old one work despite itself, in making these going corrections explicit, and in attempting a coherent synthesis of technique which gives due attention to the juice informing both the old ideology and its needed evasion. For there are few troubles with the work or theory of any lawman for which some other lawman has not by now found a shrewd, practical correction. The difficulty with jurisprudence has been not poverty, but scattering of the profusion of its wealth. Its best, gathered together, makes a rather noble showing.

Precision of legal rule according to this older ideal makes powerful appeal. Frederick the Great had his lawyers try it, writing his Code down into a detail that was to bar out all discretion of a judge and to let any man read plain what was his right.[1] The effort failed. And lawyers, proud of their art, love the alleged remark of Napoleon when he heard of the first Commentary on that Code which bears not merely his name but his handiwork: that the commentary spelt [the Code's] doom. European jurists have had long experience in the search for this type of precision, and what is no less important, with efforts to work under sets of rules which were meant to be thus precise and which were treated in fact by many of the lawmen as having accomplished that purpose. The result has been Ihering's ridicule of a discipline of empty legal concepts,[2] a general rejection of the idea of law as a "science of pure words," the flowering of a gardenful of different methods of achieving creative solution, each one a rationale for reading meaning into legal rules instead of reading meaning out of them. The lesson for us is clear. Stated cautiously, it is: there is at least one kind of certainty and precision which cannot be had consistently by way of rules of law in a world like Nineteenth and twentieth Century Europe; and too great an approximation of that kind of certainty and precision comes at an outrageous cost in social discomfort.[3]

If I read the matter aright, the kind of precision which the Europeans sought for and failed to find was what I shall call rule-of-thumb precision.[4]

1. [Jeremy Bentham had similar aspirations, and for similar reasons. His distrust of judges, part of what he saw as a self-interested conspiracy of lawyers and judges and labeled "Judge & Co.," led him to scorn judicial discretion and despise the common law. When he proposed, in all seriousness, that it should be a crime to give legal advice for money, it was in the service of creating the incentives for Parliament to write laws with sufficient clarity and precision that neither lawyers nor judicial discretion would be necessary.]

2. [Rudolf von Jhering (also spelled Ihering), *Der Kampf ums Recht* (1872), translated as *Law as a Means to an End* (Isaac Husik, trans, Boston Book 1913).]

3. [As Llewellyn suggests, increasing recognition of the impossibility of the pure civil law ideal has led actual civil law jurisdictions to take on some of the attributes of common law systems. At the same time, however, a parallel recognition in common law countries of the dangers of excess reliance on common law decision making and judge-made law has led those countries increasingly to adopt detailed statutes rather than rely on judges to develop the law in incremental fashion. And thus it is now a commonplace among comparativists to talk about the increasing *convergence* of common law and civil law approaches. See, for example, Katharina Pistor, *The Standardization of Law and Its Effect on Developing Economies*, 50 Am J Comp L 97 (2002).]

4. [As noted in the Introduction, Llewellyn's use of "rule of thumb" is idiosyncratic. The term commonly refers to a rough-and-ready heuristic that guides action if better information is not available, but has no decisional weight in its own right. And that is why writers in the act-

The words of the rules were to be so shaped that raw fact just fitted into them; it might take a trained jurist to see the fit, but even so, the goal was rule-of-thumb precision at least for a trained jurist. This is an ideal which, as has been said, rests on the machinery of formal logic, with the concepts worked out and defined in advance to exhaust any undistributed middle; and being an ideal about rules to cover the states of fact which arise in an existing world, it rests on the concepts being adequately worked out in advance to cover any state of fact which may arise in such a world. If the world would stay stable long enough to let experience accumulate, one could envisage a profession of wide men who with the help of written records could do a very respectable job on sizing up the significant categories, stating their attributes, and providing a workable set of rules to cover them. Stability, knowledge, wisdom in finding the significant, and skill in determining consequence and in phrasing; these are the necessary factors. That the human qualities concerned are indeed to be had in large measure is evidenced by the continental codes, some of which have done an astonishingly fine job in this direction; and we must remember always that a legal system does not require to be perfect or even close to perfection; over most of the field of law the various relevant portions of society have proved their ability from time to time to absorb considerable Procrustean hospitality from the law. What has given trouble is rather the matter of stability. The pace of an industrial civilization, its ongoing regroupings of interest, people, and problem, have presented new states of fact too rapidly for knowledge to keep up with them. What is more troubling, these regroupings have disturbed and thrown into doubt the *significance* of the very lines of classification on which the would-be precise rules have been made to rest. Not even the most learned, nor the most skilful, have proved able to meet that movement with a rule-of-thumb precision laid down in advance. Nor would they be able to, though they were prophets.

For the nature of rule-of-thumb classification of cases—and it is the precise ascription of the raw case to its class, and so to its legal consequence, which is the heart of this matter—the nature of such classification is that problems of the *purpose* of the classification, the *reason* of the classification,

---

utilitarian tradition are willing to accept rules of thumb, recognizing that if there is information about the consequences of a particular act that leads to a different result than that indicated by the rule of thumb, then the rule of thumb should not be followed. See Frederick Schauer, *Playing By the Rules: A Philosophical Examination of Rule-Based Decision-Making in Law and in Life* 4–5, 104–11 (Clarendon/Oxford 1991); J.J.C. Smart, *Extreme and Restricted Utilitarianism*, 6 Phil Q 344 (1956). Llewellyn's use of the term to refer to rules exactly defined and exactly fitting their purposes is at least orthogonal to and possibly even directly contradictory of standard usage.]

the *use or value* of the classification, can be disregarded in using the rule because they have been solved and left behind.[5] This is the meaning of a rule-of-thumb: it is not a rule of judgment or for judgment, it is a rule which dispenses with judgment, its meaning is the same for all officials who are supra-morons. Judgment, the rarest and most precious of judgment, is indeed needed for the initial framing of good rules of thumb, precisely because none is to be needed in their use; and for that same reason a change in conditions which throws the rule's underlying theory out of gear with the situation in hand turns a rule of thumb into a rule of thumb-fingeredness.[6] Now effective rules of thumb direct with precision that one state of fact be dealt with thus and another thus. To be good, and to satisfy, they must *rest upon* a significant and satisfying discrimination and criterion. Cases which have been seen, cases which were known when the rules were framed, *all* such cases, can by the set of rules and concepts be adequately and unmistakeably caught into the verbal frame. Indeed—and this is one nub—this *can* be done by reference to attributes which have no necessary relation to the purpose of the classification at all, and the names and nature of which shed no light on the reason for the discrimination; and what is more, description along such lines is frequently enough no mark of the rule-framer's having mistaken the accidental for the essential, but it is a neat technical device to speed business, which speeds it well so long as the kind of state of fact which bobs up does not too greatly change. Let me illustrate. Early English law knew a rule that you paid your debt in the presence of some official witnesses or your debt just was not paid. That was a rule of thumb, and, I have always thought, an admirable one. It did away with difficult disputes of fact; it provided and effective way of cleaning up transactions among men who could neither read nor write, a way easy to know of, easy to use, difficult to abuse. But it depended upon certain condition, among which were that debts and their payment be not too frequent to be remembered well and easily, that settlement was not called for at odd times and places inconvenient to access of staid official witnesses, and that the conveniences of written record be not available as an alternative. Let these presupposes conditions shift, and the excellent early English rule of thumb may still

5. [This is a crucial sentence, recognizing that taking rules (what Llewellyn calls "rules-of-thumb") seriously entails cutting off access to the reasons behind those rules in making decisions. And that is why strong forms of rule-based decision making run the risk of producing rule-based decisions that are at odds with the justifications lying behind a rule.]

6. ["Thumb-fingeredness" appears to be Llewellyn's neologism for heavy-handedness, clumsiness, or, in the case of rules, insufficient fit between a rule's literal application and its background purposes.]

work law, but it will promptly work either inconvenience or injustice as a price. *In itself,* however, it provides no machinery for its own proper modification or revamping, if conditions shift. The nature of a rule-of-thumb is to run free, in its expression, of its purpose.

Let us not stay wholly with the ancient ways. We have a rule of thumb today about indorsement of a negotiable promissory note due in the future. When the payee and owner sells the note in advance of maturity, he commonly indorses it to the buyer, and the indorsement amounts, roughly, to his assurance that the note is safe to buy from his because he will pay it if the maker for any reason fails to do. Now most persons who hold such paper want their money at maturity, and proceed to present the paper promptly for payment; most makers of such paper, moreover, are jealous of their credit and are ready to meet the paper when it falls due. These facts, and the normal expectations which result therefrom, lie behind a certain rule of thumb in which the facts and their meaning, of course, find no expression. The rule is this: that if the holder of the paper does not present it properly for payment on the precise day of maturity, the indorser who sold it to him is no longer bound, but is discharged. It makes no difference that no loss was in fact suffered by the non-presentment, because, say, the note was payable at a bank, and the maker had no credit there, and presentment was made to the maker himself the following day, and he did not fail until two weeks thereafter. It makes no difference that he had stopped payment a month before the note fell due. It is the flattest rule-of-thumb style of rule of law. Unlike the early English rule mentioned above, it is not a wholly satisfying one, it is one only rough-carpentered to fit the area it covers; and, as so often, the lawmen's other and semi-corrective ways show their appreciation of this. For a business-man who, against reliance on his own standing, took full value for the note may well feel a failure of presentment which has caused no loss to be a less than honest excuse for a discharge; he may say: "Don't worry; I will make it good." If he does, then his promise will stick, and be enforceable. What makes this stand out as an attempted correction of our rule of thumb is that our system of law knows very few situations indeed in which even a business man's business promise made without an agreed return is binding in law because of its mere making. The "anomaly" here engrafted on the general requirement of "consideration" for a promise thus softens the rule of thumb in one class of case which falls outside its reason. But the engraftment does not wholly cure the maladjustment. It is a makeshift upon a makeshift, because the reason for discharging the indorser at all is not reflected in the rule of thumb, and so the rule's failure to fit the situation neatly does not appear sharply, and challenges to clean and thorough recarpentry.[7] What we have is a helter skelter patch slapped on a sloppy job. Before leaving this rule on indorser-discharge one may note another thing, the use of external marks to guide use of rules of thumb. The element important in the early English rule was discharge of a debt by payment; but the mark fixed on was the witnessing of payment by certain officials; the mark was not identical with the substance, but it lay so close, that in the economy of the time it could be made for practical purposes to coincide. Nonetheless, it was the mark, not the substance, on which the rule of thumb was hinged. In the indorser-discharge rule the substance is loss of collection from the note's maker, loss due to sloth of the holder; the mark selected again lies close, but nowhere near so close; and the legal consequence, total discharge, when attached to failure of the mark, is flat and crude. This is not because a properly chosen mark may not serve the purpose of a rule of thumb, though it may have even less internal connection with the substance; the trouble here is that the mark is, as the facts run, too frequently off the mark. Not in the run of transactions and collections, which are well guided by men's interest in getting money in, and which acquire a further touch of help and guidance from the rule; but in the run of defaults, to which the rule is peculiarly addressed.

I hope it will be clear that I am not waging war on certain and precise rules. What I am trying to do is to show what the utility of the rule-of-thumb style of rule is, and what that utility is not. Indeed, by turning to an intimately related rule drawn from the same semi-code (the Uniform Negotiable Instruments Law) we can illustrate another type of rule-drafting which works upon a wholly different theory and with a wholly different technique. I shall call it the technique of *explicit principle,* as distinct from the technique of rule-of-thumb. Its essence lies in that it articulates the *reason* of the rule, and incorporates the reason into the rule itself. Its effect is to provide open-endedness. It leaves the rule free to meet new conditions with *guidance;* it *presses* the variant official personnel *toward* resolving questions on new emergent fact along similar lines, or even the same lines; it *enables* them, under the use and guidance of the rule itself, to solve such problems in a satisfying fashion. One requires to be neither a logician nor a semanticist to see and feel the difference in approach and the difference in effect. Nor does the difference require to be intentional in the framer of the rule; it is enough that a happy stroke of phrasing effect the result. We can see this, I think, in the rule I have in mind, which is that on presentment not of time notes,

7. [This awkward phrase seems to suggest that poorly drafted rules of thumb will require frequent adjustment and frequent redrafting—hence the word "recarpentry."]

but of checks: if a *check* is unduly delayed in presentment, the drawer of the check is discharged not utterly, but *to the extent of the loss caused by the delay*. It is moderately clear that the framers of the Negotiable Instruments Law did not sit down to draw two different types of rule to cover the two cases. The cases are in underlying purpose closely similar. Both seek to make it a holder's risk to "use due diligence" to collect outstanding negotiable paper from the person who normally can be expected to pay it; both, if such diligence be used, assume that he who passed the paper for full value must make it good, and take over the burden and possible loss of wrestling with the person who failed to pay it as expected. The difference lies not in purpose but in history. The note rule had become a rule of thumb before the framers of the Negotiable Instruments Law began their work, and it came to them buttressed by a certain decency in its application to an indorser who had gone on the paper not as an incident to selling it, but as an accom[m]odation to his friend, the maker. The check rule, on the other hand, was of relatively recent and independent origin; deposit banking was no old institution, failure of banks was heavily in mind, the danger of such failure to a drawer who froze his account to keep cover ready for outstanding checks was clear. The new type of risk, deposit credit left in bank, being in mind, was expressed, in "loss caused by the delay"; expressed not as a general idea, illuminating the field, but as a special incident of the check, whose peculiar purpose and developing law were fresh in mind. It is moderately clear, I say, that there was no design to draft a rule of thumb in the one case, a rule containing explicit principle in the other. Yet the fresh memory of why the check rule had come to be, marked its expression with words of limitation to its purpose. So that *if* the drawer does as a decent drawer keep credit there available at his bank, and *if* the bank fails and pays less than 100 cents on the deposits, then to the extent of the loss the properly acting drawer is discharged as against a holder who let presentment go until the bank had stopped honoring checks. No man can quarrel with this. But neither can any man read the check-rule without being *reminded* of its reason, nor can he try to apply the check-rule without remembering that reason. So that when situations arose more recently which the draftsmen of the N.I.L. were certainly not envisaging in 1897, and bank deposits came under insurance or guaranty, there was moderate guidance at hand in the rule itself to offer the wherewithal to absorb and cope with the new variant situation.

As a first distinction, then, within the field of rules of law to be expressed in the form of propositions prescribing the legal consequence of a described type of situation of fact, let us note as at one pole the rule-of-thumb, in which the flat result is articulated, leaving behind and unexpressed all indication of its reason; and let us note as at the other pole the way of principle, in which the reason is clearly and effectively articulated, and that articulation is made part of the very rule.[8] Most current rules will be found mixed of the two elements; the one prevailing here, the other there; and we shall see that the two lines of approach call for differences in language machinery, and conceptual machinery, and in the structure of the rule. Rules of thumb, for instance, consort most happily with detail, with narrow range, with circumscribed as well as prescribed legal consequence, and with use of external signs to mark their application, whereas the vice of principle can be a vaporish vagueness, and the techniques of its effective formulation are not easy to isolate for communication and use. But of that hereafter. The point here is that a stable closed universe of states of fact, and concepts skilfully built to fit that world, and turned to use by formal logic of the schoolmen's type,[9] is the ideal world to which the rule-of-thumb type of rule of law is perfectly adopted. A next point is that such an ideal and such a logic pulse through our own legal system as *one* of its main currents, and feed especially that part of legal work we know as "legal reasoning." The last point, to sum up this part of the discussion, is to repeat that the European attempts to cope with the problems of their law on such a basis have shattered of necessity upon the shifting character of modern conditions. It is thus in regard to their emergent problems, their emergent groupings, their emergent new significances that we find the continentals developing their construction by analogy, or opening and widening their gaps-in-the-law (that is, in the *rules* of law) to fill up with what we should call judicial legislation, or construing "as the legislat[or] would have meant it if he were speaking today and to this problem", or sizing up and weighing the interests typically at state, as a guide to "interpretation"—that we find them, in a word, escaping limitation by the word, and using their rules rather as guides than as either compulsions or limitations. Thus it seems a sound generalization from their experi-

8. [Modern readers may be inclined to think that Llewellyn's distinction between rule of thumb and explicit principle tracks the contemporary terminology of rules and standards, but that is not quite right. Standards are understood as vague and flexible, incorporating terms like "reasonable" and "with due cause" in order to give the applier of a rule the freedom to adapt the rule to changing circumstances or unexpected facts. But although Llewellyn's explicit principles might well be similarly vague or open-ended, they need not be. A precise rule with a precisely expressed and incorporated reason—"works of art being unique, breach of a contract to deliver a work of art shall be enforced by specific performance"—is far too precise to qualify as a standard under the modern terminology, but by providing its own background justification would ensure that perverse applications—requiring specific performance in the case of a work with one thousand identical copies readily available on the open market—would be avoided.]

9. [The reference here to "schoolmen" is best understood as a reference to medieval scholasticism, and its accompanying reputation for almost pointless formality and precision.]

ence to say that when the problems or the facts change form and meaning fast enough so that what reformulation-machinery the system offers cannot be expected to keep up, then rule-of-thumb precision is no optimum for the relevant rule. Too much of it, under those conditions, invites—nay, seeks to force—a rule to work results which, though they fit its language, yet either shock its own implicit reason or, if its reason also be outdate[d], then just shock reason. Under such circumstances, even case-hardened literal-minded judges squirm; and experience shows that squirming judges mean uncertain and unpredictable results, as sense of general decency in result rolls in its wrestle with sense of legal decency in rule-work. Finally, we have seen that irregularity of result means imprecision in the *positive* rule of law. Its partial positivity then belies its certain form: no optimum there.

But it would be shallow scanning of the continental rules which took their storm-centers as their whole. Two decades after "Gnaeus Flavius" burst into the cry for "free law," for a reaching outside the words of statutory rules to find the just decision, we find the same Kantorowic[z], now without pseudonym, seeking to arrange the use of materials from outside the words of rules into an ordered and verbalized dogmatic scheme, technique and hierarchy.[10] That may reflect in minor part a personal advance in age and position; vastly more, it evidences the legal system in question producing its own lines of balance on the question.

10. [Llewellyn is referring to *Der Kampf um die Rechtswissenschaft*, published in 1906 by Hermann Ulrich Kantorowicz (1877–1940) (Llewellyn misspelled the name as "Kantorowich") under the pseudonym "Gnaeus Flavius." This and other works of the Free Law School—*Freirechtsschule*—are often considered as important precursors of American Legal Realism. See James E. Herget and Stephen Wallace, *The German Free Law Movement as the Source of American Legal Realism*, 73 Va L Rev 399 (1987).]

CHAPTER V

Rule of Conduct, and the Legal Order

It is now time to turn to one approach to the idea of rules of law which we may seem to have been scanting, one which, like each other approach to which honest thinkers have been led, will prove to back its good load of insight and utility. I refer to the conception of a rule of law as being in essence a *rule of conduct*. For our purposes the possible twists which this central notion may give to such other attributes as positivity, authority, sanction attached and sanction limited, can be left on one side; for we do not propose to make this approach to the rule of law our own, but only to milk it for what it can add to our own.

"Rule of conduct" is indeed a concept too fluid and at the same time too muddy to serve as a satisfactory tool for an analysis of the technical work of rules of law; it is an amalgam rather than a unity; but one of the elements in that amalgam is one which any concept of rule of law needs to take account of.[1] That element is the reference to and insistence on the ways in which *people* go round, the patterns of behavior, the patterns of group-organization, the patterns of idea prevalent about what behavior is and what groups are, and what each is for, and what each should be and should be for. These things enter into rules of positive law. They grind the lenses through which the profession sees the words of rules. They shape professional intuition about what in a rule makes sense, what kind of sense it makes, how far to follow a premise and when to drop it, when to reshape it, when to go looking for a variant premise or even an opposing one.

Insofar as "rule of conduct" contains the idea "rule *for* conduct[,]" it partakes of the nature of command, or of that conditional, cook-book style

1. [See Meir Dan-Cohen, *Decision Rules and Conduct Rules: Acoustic Separation in Criminal Law*, 97 Harv L Rev 625 (1984).]

of direction which lays down that *if* you want an effective testamentary disposition, the way to get one is as follows, etc. We can pass over one implicit limitation in the "rule of conduct" formula: that so far as it prescribes, it prescribes not merely a state of mind or soul, but some conduct which the State-machine can deal with; and that it differs in this from a purely "moral precept." What we cannot pass over, in this "rule *for* conduct" phase, is the emphasis on the citizen or subject rather than on any official, as being the addressee of the rule. Of course the implicit command to any relevant judge or other official, which we have made part of our propositional form of rule, is present in the rule *for* conduct idea, too, so far as any such rule is accompanied by any specified sanction of reward or threat; and where the rule deals immediately with the organization and running of the State-machine itself, these officials of one sort or another may be the direct addressees of the dominant direction or command. But the bulk-weight of the rule *for* conduct aspect rests on the subject or the citizen; the rule is seen as there to make him go round, as a command would be. But what is more, the very fact that "rule *for* conduct" is only one aspect of "rule *of* conduct," and is one which we have to analyze out in order to see it, points the essential difference from the command approach. The rule is here seen, by the mere phrasing (as a command is not easily seen)[,] as not only *to* make the subject or citizen go round and go round in a given way, but *as accomplishing that result*: it is a rule *of* his conduct.

The way is tricky in which all this is held together conceptually, and held together also with the patent fact of variant conduct there to be observed, and held together also, by some daring spirits, with the idea of rules of law as something limited to their indicated legal consequence. The best I can do to describe it is this: a "rule *of* conduct" (as a positive rule of law) implies first a positive rule *for* conduct, with a sanction and a purpose. It implies[,] second, a going *practice* among the bulk of relevant subjects or citizens which conforms to the purpose of the rule and which is commonly so arranged in detail as either to keep conduct out of technical contact with the afflictive sanctions or to enlist the rewarding sanctions at need,[2] and with technical efficiency. It implies, third, a going recognition among the subjects or

2. [When Llewellyn was writing, the prevailing Austinian theory of law treated commands backed by the threat of negative (what Llewellyn calls "afflictive") sanctions—punishments or fines—as genuine law, but refused to recognize the promise of rewards as a genuine legal sanction. John Austin, *The Province of Jurisprudence Determined* (Wilfrid E. Rumble, ed, Cambridge 1995) (1832). Llewellyn clearly was having none of this, and here recognized explicitly that law functioned as often and as effectively by the promise of rewards as by the threat of punishment.]

citizens at large that such conforming conduct is legal conduct and variant conduct runs counter to law, and that the technical results ought, if all were as it should be, to follow as of course; ideally, moreover, (and it is probably safe to say; unless contrary is explicit) it implies that conforming conduct is right and infringing conduct is wrong. If my understanding of these implications is correct, then the "rule of conduct" idea embodies all the virtues and defects of layman's thinking about law, as against professional thinking. It is blurred precisely where the professional needs sharpened focus, to wit on the exact relation of what is *felt* as conforming or non-conforming conduct to what will be done or can be done about the matter by the State-machine. When a lawyer uses this approach, he presupposes just what it is [that it is] a lawyer's professional business not to presuppose but to check up on: to wit, that conduct *felt* to conform to purpose will produce the technical results which also are in question. The approach plays up *purpose* not in the fashion of a technician but in that of a folk-philosopher. A Will Rogers,[3] for instance, lets no technical didoes[4] stand between his perception of discrepancy between what is wanted and what is produced; he punctures self-satisfied soap bubblings with his quiet queries into just where it gets you or what it[']s all about, or he touches up some obvious discrepancy which makes you grin—and then wonder. This folk-philosopher's approach renders unto rules of law that general presumption of rightness which in general idea they do carry; but it spits with tolerant skepticism over whether any given one of them, what with the technicalities, the lawyers and the politicians, can be made to give the "law-abiding" citizen his due. It refuses utterly to be befuddled by any hard-eyed chiseller who has hired a Philadelphia lawyer to keep him where "the law can't touch him" (and the meaning of "the law" shifts, as that phrase comes to mind.) Its feet, in a word, are planted in the soil, not in the courts; it is an unanalyzed concept which goes indeed to one major essential of "the law," but does not go to the technical problems of technicians getting particular action out of other technicians by way of *rules* of law. It gives no hold for hand or foot when the problem is how to draw a rule which will, within our given technical frame, move the man who must be moved in such manner as to *accomplish* the result desired.

3. [Will Rogers (1879–1935) was a popular actor and humorist of Llewellyn's time, noteworthy for saying, among other things, "I never met a man I didn't like." Presumably Llewellyn is using the name to describe an ordinary plain-thinking everyman imbued with commonsense even if lacking in technical training.]

4. [A "didoes" (singular) is a prank, trick, or antic, and in this context might be understood to refer to a clever machination.]

But these are no reasons for disregarding the concept of "rule of conduct" in relation to the technical measure. In the first place, the concept gathers rather admirably our prevailing folk-concept of rule of law—which is a queer blend of "the law" in general. "[T]he law" somehow applied to a situation, and any half-understood particular technical rule which may be lying around, with cloudy "purposes" felt at once as part of "the law" and as at odds with its technique or personnel. And that folk-concept, including a vague tolerance and approval, a willingness to conform passively if it is not *too* inconvenient, a willingness if roused to back any part for the whole's sake, and regardless of who may get hurt—that is part of the background for all technique of the technicians. So is the non-universality of the folk-picture; the fact, for instance, that *some* of the people are shrewd law-consumers who have learned to deal with the law-machine on its purely technical side. But above all, this folk-concept requires our notice because we lawyer-technicians ourselves began as members of the undifferentiated folk, and have not at all gotten over that fact; let us nod for a moment, or let us be baffled, or let us come under heavy pressure of work, or let us get into an area where the lines of technical guidance which any one of us happens to have had most to do with fail him, and the lay half of any one of us will make itself felt with force upon his technical work itself. If you have doubt, because you feel the technical ways to verge on second nature, then watch a lawyer thirty years trained to distrust ex parte evidence, to demand a hearing, to explore the possibilities of cross-examination, to manipulate publicity—watch that same lawyer make up his mind on the basis of one more untested newspaper report, and go to cursing like a layman on almost any matter in which he is *not* thinking for a client.[5] No; each lawman—and in good part that is fortunate—is a layman still, as well. Nor is that the only reason for keeping an eye out to the layman's concept of the law. For one of the effects of going on the bench, and of being thereby removed from the practitioner's pressure to see it as *purely a technical matter, in his client's interest,* is to give the lawyer-mounting-the-bench a fresh injection of this folk-approach. The essen[c]e of that approach is horse-sense; is interest as to purpose and result, in order that techniques may work horse-sense; is live intuition that techniques as measured by a public or a judge must be *for* something, and that the product of techniques and rules ought to be some rough justice in adjudication. There is *balance* to be felt and to be felt for,

5. [It is not entirely clear whether Llewellyn intends this observation as a comment on the wise sophistication of the lawyer, which he or she occasionally forgets, or instead on the intrinsic artificiality of legal thinking.]

balance the feeling for which is derived from how people go round and how people size things up—from their "rules of conduct," in the fullest implication of that phrase. Such factors work on and in the judge as they do not work on and in the lawyer who has his row of clients to keep his technical vision at its sharpest and most conscious, and it is the judge whose work determines with authority just what the technical measures mean.[6]

So much truth and solidity is there [in] this "rule of conduct" idea, and so delicate is the passage of the given conduct-patterns and the given ideology about proper conduct through the capillaries and into the bloodstream of the technical rules, that there is little wonder either that profound thinkers could see in this phase *the* life and essence of "law," or that they could turn to semi-mysticism in attempting to account for the processes of the growth and change. It is not my desire to enter in this book upon any discussion of the nature of "law" or of "the law"; the book has enough to do in wrestling with our rules of law, our technical measures, as they shape and work between our ideals on the one hand and our going legal institutions on the other. But it will help somewhat to see the full worthwhileness of the "rule of conduct" concept as that worthwhileness was caught into the work of the best Germans and has not been caught into the phrasing of their translators or imitators in our tongue, if we note that "rule" in the phrase is a poor word, a word of poverty. "Rightful way of conduct" comes closer to the underlying concept; and even there, the phrasing is too singular, too sharp. "Of conduct" belongs properly together with a plural, a plural conceived as an organized, interlocking, *un*analyzed unity of parts, each dependent for its meaning on its relation to the whole: *Recht* in the sense of a German of the Thirteenth Century, as recaptured by the historical jurists (say Gierke),[7] and as still current where the speech has not been run through a modern juridical cooler—Recht in this sense Englishes as "characteristic and rightful way of life": one *lives* the Recht of the Saxons, he does not live under it; it is indeed *his* Recht. Writers like Puchta[8] have been criticized for confusing law, morals and custom; and it is true that their writings do. But their less patient critics have not spotted the lines of cause of the confusion. In reaching for

6. [Note the difference here between Llewellyn's view that the judge and the lawyer have markedly different mindsets, and Jerome Frank's view in *Law and the Modern Mind* (Brentano's 1930) that judges are fundamentally like lawyers with clients, both starting with a commitment to some outcome and then looking for the arguments and authorities that will support that preselected outcome.]

7. [Otto von Gierke (1841–1921), author of, most prominently, *Political Theories of the Middle Ages* (Frederic William Maitland, trans, Cambridge 1900).]

8. [Georg Friedrich Puchta (1798–1846), a prominent German commentator on Roman law.]

the Volksgeist such writers did not *con*fuse, but *fused*, things which in a modern society possessed of a modern State machine have become conceptually quite distinct, and have become practically distinct enough to give point to the conceptual distinction. But the fusion was sound procedure, for a starter[.] When they then sought to de-fuse, they picked as the critical marks of "law" something other than the marks proper to our modern society and conceptual system; again, in dealing with a different society, a sound procedure. Such analysis well serves anthropology, and serves legal history well, and indeed serves the study of the control machinery of modern society and of the very State machine within it, when a control machinery is being studie[d] *as a whole*. The *con*fusion lay in applying the results of such an analysis, almost without modification, to specifically technical phases of modern law: to modern State-backed rules and their work. It is because Ehrlich[9] cleanly isolated the technical machine for separate study that he represents such an advance over Puchta; it is because [Frederick William] Maitland concentrated on King's law, not on *the* law of medieval England, that his work neither itself displayed the confusion nor yet made plain to others how to clear it up; it is because Max Weber perceived that the technical problems of the State rules and machine have their analogues throughout the other groupings of a modern society, and that a society is built not only of a people but of a complex of interacting groupings of people that his Sociology of Law so far outstrips anything else in print.

All of this it is needful to set out because some "rule of conduct" thinkers have carried their insight through, and have carried a confusion of language through together with it, into the concept of "the legal order." And we need both to get the juice out of that concept and to get rid of those of its connotations which for us would be misleading. Recht in the German folk sense which we have mentioned is of itself a whole *order*: an order which, among other aspects, has also its legal aspects in any sense in which one wishes to use that word. But Recht in 19th century Germany was also a term of art among professional lawmen, and a term with many meanings. Rechts *ordnung*, then, picked up with a peculiarly professional flavor the idea of a total régime, and gave it also that twist of "*controlled* by technical rules of law" which runs with the "rule of conduct" way of thinking, and left it then for us to English into "legal order." The notion is clear that what is being talked of is a product of technical measures and their personnel; the notion of

9. [Eugen Ehrlich (1862–1922), an Austrian legal theorist who was one of the leading early figures in the so-called sociological school of jurisprudence. A brief but useful description is in Edwin W. Patterson, *Jurisprudence: Men and Ideas of the Law* 79–82 (Foundation 1953).]

an ongoing ordering is implicit; the notion is of a pervasive régime, which includes both a condition and a process, with technical measures and their personnel as *the* potently and immediately causative factors. The trouble for our purposes is that so much of the order and ordering of society as works apart from, or in addition to, or at cross-purposes with, the technical measures and their personnel, gets lost in the shuffle, and gets implicitly attributed to the "legal" aspects of the order. Nor are we greatly helped by such a fuller phrasing as "a régime of the direction of politically organized society," because "politically organized society" unifies and lumps just those two aspects: the technical rules and *their* people, and what *else* there may be of ordering, which we need to keep distinct in thought, that the two may be seen more sharply in their interaction.

We shall therefore accept the notion of an *order* of society; and we shall add the notion that parts of society may have each its order. But we shall regard these orders—in their due combination of given condition and ongoing process—as being "legal" only insofar as we can observe that they are made or shaped or controlled by rules of law or by ideas about rules of law or by action of the officials of the State-machine. The choice of terms is dictated by our problem. It implies no position in the battle-royal about what "law" may be. It is an effort to find a vocabulary which can deal with what we require to deal with, without danger or confusion, no matter what a reader's beliefs—or a writer's—may be upon that much debated question.

For we need the distinction between the technical stuff and the order of society. Their relation is not unlike that between conscious action and habit in an individual. Faced with a need for conscious action, the individual certainly is hugely shaped in his reaction and in his conscious choice by his existing habit-structure. Out of the conscious choice or action may grow then another habit, incorporated duly into a habit-structure somewhat altered by the incorporation. That each aspect influences the other does not do away with the value of distinguishing between them. Neither do we see that *all* habits rest on any conscious prior choice. Somewhat of this nature is the play of the order of society upon the rules of law, and the play of the rules of law upon that order.

Yet a *legal order* we do have, and there is no mistaking that fact. It may not be the effective order of our world, but the effective order of our technical world of rules of law it is. It is an institutional and ideological order. It consists of the ways in which the men of the law do things, and see things, and think things, and of the ways into which these other ways are cogged and locked into patterns and these in turn into greater patterns. It is an "order" because it is there, and is a whole, and taken men in and shapes them in its image, and accommodates such of their work as it does not dictate. It is above all an "order" because it is not reduced to words, but shapes them as well as its people. From the order of society, which includes all of positive law and positive law's work together with so much else, and from the legal phases of that order of society, let me then distinguish the order of the technical world of positive law, a vast enough corpus in all conscience, but at least one with a discernible center and a guessable border-zone.[10] Part of this order are those thought-ways and action-ways of the profession which fight shy of fixing out rules of law too tightly by any verbal pegs. Part of it is the judge-centeredness of our legal ideology. Part of it is the absence of any Supreme Court of Common Law, with a resultant democratic process of competition among courts and among announced rules for influence and, as to the rules, even for survival.[11] Part of it are our institutions of the signed opinion and of the published dissent, which officially stress, to the dismay of the continental lawyer, that our legal order not only officially recognizes the play of personality and the absence of complete control of judgment by the rules, but proposes to gather value from the recognition.

The part of that order of the technical legal world which concerns us immediately is found in the classifications of the law. I speak not of proposals as to how most wisely to classify the law for reference and for use; I speak of classifications which, wise or unwise, useful or wasteful, pertinent or silly, are simply there. They are given, they are institutionally given, there are shapes and groupings in which things *are* sized up, and other ways in which they are *not* sized up. These shapes and groupings we do not make, but take; they are the air we breathe as we grow up into the profession, they are part of the *nature* of our law. What is more, and what for my immediate purpose is much worse, we have gotten so used to these classifications, we think in terms of them so readily, so automatically, so inescapably, that it irks to be asked to stop and think about them. Men are not interested in talking or thinking of the technique of walking unless they have trouble using their

10. [Note the similarity to H.L.A. Hart's view that specific rules have clear cores of straightforward application and vague penumbras requiring interpretive discretion. H.L.A. Hart, *Positivism and the Separation of Law and Morals*, 71 Harv L Rev 593, 606–15 (1958). For discussion and analysis of the point, see Frederick Schauer, *A Critical Guide to Vehicles in the Park*, 83 NYU L Rev 1109 (2008).]

11. [On the way in which the multiplicity of American jurisdictions, arranged nonhierarchically for common law issues, makes the rule-skeptical aspect of Legal Realism especially plausible, see Brian Leiter, *Rule and Reason*, Times Literary Supplement 26 (February 12, 2010).]

legs, nor in the technique of breathing unless they face some new problem about breathing, as a singer does, or a swimmer, or a population about to be trained to the gas-mask. We walk and we breathe, in law, these given classifications, and we have no interest in discussion of them. Yet I do not see how we can gain power over rules of law without some study of them. For what we *feel* about them tricks us half as often as it helps us out; for what we "know" about them, where not inaccurate, is polka-dotted around without pattern. Yet they cut into our rules of law at every turn, with effect, but mostly without remark by them or us.

In the first place, they both shape and limit our rules. This is in part because our rules are cast in concepts which derive from these given classifications of our legal order; but it is no less because the classifications guide and limit our imaginations as to what areas are proper to be grouped at all as units for *a* rule to apply to, so that as of course we look for *a* rule for any *one* of the areas, and as of course limit the sense of any rule from any area to that area, and only under severe pressure can we be brought to reexamine the areas or their boundaries to see whether they are in fact useful units for our rules of law to be about. The classifications do not of course stay put, forever; but as of any given moment or even generation they are put, [and] they are put [ ] hard.

Take Tort and Contract. It is beside the point that Contract today centers on the informal contract which once was the subject of a form of suit known as assumpsit which once was a form of suit known as action on the case which we recognize as being of the genus known as Tort. What is to the point today is that acquired a different putness of Tort and Contract; the two have acquired a distinctive and even disjunctive character; the easy way to define a Tort is to start out in terms of a private and civil wrong other than a breach of contract. If a rule is about the one, then it is not about the other; we must allow suits to be brought in which "counts in tort and contract are joined", that is, in which the plaintiff sets forth the facts of a transaction now to make out a case we recognize as breach of contract and again to make out a case under this "other" type of duty labelled with the Law French name for wrong. And a principle of civil damages is not to be read as a principle of damages, but there will be one rule for cases of Contract and another for cases of Tort. And a consumer injured by a defective gas heater or bad food has available two quite different bodies of rules of law, with both possibilities and limitations that are irreconcilable in sense; for the one body of rules happens to be built on the rules of "negligence", which is Tort, and the other on the rules of "warranty", and that is Contract, so that it is not yet, after half a century of experience with the problem, feasible or even decent to merge the two ways of going at the matter into an effective whole. This is not because thus to dichotomize Tort and contract makes sense in application to a problem causing high over a thousand recorded appeals. It is because the classifications given by our law are as they are.

Or take a field I have labored over for some years, "the" field of Sales. Sales does not, as an uninitiated person might imagine, mean sales. It means sales of goods; sales of land have quite different rules, and I for one think they should; those rules are grouped in a different "field" known as Vendor and Purchaser. What is less fortunate, but equally given, is that the rules of sales are almost exclusively a body of rules of "law" in the stricter sense, as distinguished from that serviceable and rather more flexible body of remedy and principle known as equity—which, as the name implies, exist[s] to get done some equitable things which strict "law" may be too technical or rigid or cumbersom[e] to handle. The failure of these rules of equity to show up in the field of Sales today is little noticed, though for a field to scant them is like shackling one leg and arm; Vendor and Purchaser is for instance built upon them. But Sales will have none of them, and will not even notice that it will not; that very trust which is the heart of equity thinking, when it ventures into Sales in the form of the banker's security device known as the "trust receipt", changes its nature. This absence of equity rules and concepts has effects on Sales, and they are not happy effects; my point is that lawmen do not notice that or set about to remedy it, because as the classification Sales is *given*, so it is taken. As given, to continue, it means sales of "goods"; not sales "of personal property" which would be of everything except land, but of goods, moveable tangibles. Thus negotiable paper, book accounts, sticks, bonds, are perceived by the given classification to be significantly different from tangible goods, for purposes of sale. And so they are, and we can be thankful for the differentiation. But on the other hand, merchant to merchant sales of the wares of trade in the current of commerce are also significantly different from a farmer's selling of his new calf, and from a turning over by a boarding-house keeper of her furniture to liquidate the unpaid rent, and indeed from that sale to a consumer of the defective gas-heater spoken of above.[12] But this significant differentiation is *not* perceived by and

12. [This paragraph embodies two important Realist themes. First, it reflects the Realist penchant for smaller rather than larger legal categories; and, second, it displays the Realist preference for categories that track the categories of the extralegal world, as opposed to forcing the events of the world into the categories of the law. With respect to both of these themes, Llewellyn's characteristically Realist views are usefully contrasted with those of Holmes, who often expressed sympathy for larger and distinctively legal categories, perhaps nowhere more than in his well-known apocryphal story of the churn: "There is a story of a Vermont justice of

reflected in the given classification—nor is its absence consciously noted. True, we notice with pleasure that our general rules about sales of *tangibles* are not embarrassed in their drafting or in their "application" (which is their meaning) by the peculiarities of book account transactions or of wage assignments; or of sticks and bonds. All these are placed, like land, in some other category, and we see and admire the wisdom of the law. But that our general rules on sales in current trade, by merchants to merchants for resale which cry out for their separate regulation, *are* embarrassed by the peculiarities of farmers' sales and consumers' purchases and transfers by hounded debtors in desperate liquidation of old debts, and vice versa—that we do not see as the unwisdom of the law; we do not see it at all; we simply take the lines of "obvious" unity or difference as our technical system gives them to us. Indeed, [an] American lawyer reading this is thinking: But how else *could* you draw the lines? Or else: but we make out all right, anyhow, don't we?

To justify an answer to the second question (the answer being: No) would lead the discussion astray. But the first is answerable cheaply by recalling that both French and German law take "sales" of land and other things together, and mark off sales by merchants in their business from the lot. The point is not just what they do, nor whether it is wiser than what we do. The point is that these givers of classification, throughout the world of our rules of law, do guide and limit those rules of law in their making, and in their meaning when made. *And that as to much of that guidance and that limitation, the process is so automatic that we do not even notice it as we take part in it or are swept along by it. Of course* any rule of law in the real property field is to be given an extra dosage of rule-of-thumbishness. That has become explicit in our concept "rule of property", which means in essence a rule not to be consciously modified even when it is *seen* to be off purpose, lest its modification retroactively unsettle too many past transactions and too many present

---

the peace against whom a suit was brought by one farmer against another for breaking a churn. The justice took time to consider, and then said that he had looked through the statutes and could find nothing about churns, and gave judgment for the defendant." Oliver W. Holmes, *The Path of the Law*, 10 Harv L Rev 457, 474–75 (1897). And Holmes then goes further, making clear that for him the blunder of the Vermont justice was in thinking that the relevant categories were those of the world and not those of law: "Applications of rudimentary rules of contract or tort are [often mistakenly] tucked away under the heads of Railroads or Telegraphs or . . . Shipping . . . , or are gathered under an arbitrary title which is thought likely to appeal to the practical mind, such as Mercantile Law. If a man goes into law it pays to be a master of it, and to be a master of it means to look straight through all the dramatic incidents and to discern the true basis for prophecy." Id at 475. For analysis of the example and the issues it raises, see Frederick Schauer, *Prediction and Particularity*, 78 BU L Rev 773 (1998).]

situations which rest thereon. But the added dose of rule-of-thumbishness is present also in a less tangible *attitude* in the real property field. Specialists in the field have often exaggerated the certainty there, but surely they are entitled to their pride that property reasoning is tighter and property concepts more sharply edged than they find concepts or reasoning to be when they cross the line. The way of saying it, would be that real property is one of the very few areas in which our private-document attitude toward language is found also in our attitude toward the rules of law, both being consciously built toward a maximum of unyielding permanency. What wonder then that it shocks *of course* to find a judge reading a "commercial document with the eyes of the conveyance", or that one finds curious cross-eddoes in mortgage-law according as judges happen to have moved or been moved into the dominant gravitational sphere of property thinking, commercial thinking, or equity thinking, in a mortgage situation where the debt is commercial, the mortgage is on real estate and the proceeding is one in equity? For *of course* a commercial document is to be read with an eye to dominant intent, and perhaps even with due consideration of the unwritten background of the transaction; and of *course* any rules of equity should have the feeling of its principle kept live, and lives in conscious flux with other rules of equity. There may be equity rules which have lost touch with their principle; one of the most famous of them, that of bona fide purchase for value of the legal title, has become almost as rule-of-thumbish as the rule that sequence of time for occurrence flatly determines independence of precedent conditions; but if I might be permitted a speculation I should feel safe in gambling that the bona fide purchase rule remains wooden only because it is *believed* to state its principle, and because the principle it is believed to state is *believed* to be a good one. For while rules of equity are also subject to hardening of the arteries, they dip from time to time in youth-renewal.

What holds of such flavors in portions of the technical order holds also of aspects more directly intellectual. *Of course* the field of Contract is *agreements*, unless it happens *of course* to be promises (and the field will look very different, according to which is "of course"); but in neither case are family transactions to be distinguished (save perhaps as to the beneficiary rules) from business transactions, nor the initiation of business transactions from their going readjustment, nor form-pad printings from individuated writings, nor the internal arrangements of a business unit from deals between business units. And *of course* an offer is for *either* a bilateral *or* a unilateral. *Of course* closely held business corporations and those built to invite investment by the public are subject to the same rules—barring Blue Sky Commissions[13] and the [Securities and Exchange Commission]. *Of course* a mortgage presupposes a debt, and extends only to a fixed interest in a fixed asset. *Of course* the rules of a single Negotiable Instruments Law, drawn on the model of individual pieces of short-term clean commercial paper, cover also those banknotes which used to pass as cash, bankers' collateral notes, and thirty year investment mortgage bonds in series; but *checks* (almost alone) have their several needed and peculiar rules—and equally as *of course,* because they have.

Such are the moulds into which the given order of our technical world, unnoticed, relentless, presses rules and presses the classifications on which our rules depend, and presses our lawmen's ideas of *what to look for* in a situation. For rules of law take the three-dimensional multicolored situation of raw fact and light it from a single angle and in a single color, that of the *legally significant.* And as the same hills are different hills at high noon or in the westering red[14] or in twilight or moonlight, so the same raw fact-situation changes form and meaning and even content according to the legal lighting which picks out this for emphasis, and leaves that dark, or irrelevant, or intrusive. If Miss Elsie Jones, factory efficiency expert, in private life Mrs. Robert Andrews, is driving her Buick to work on the right side of the state road at 45 m.p.h., the legally significant aspects of that situation might have been, a thousand years ago, that she was within a peculiar Peace of the King because on a peculiar "high"way; and five hundred years ago it might have been that she was manipulating a witches' vehicle: Today in modern England it may be that she is on the wrong side of the road; or in Massachusetts that she has registered the Buick in her "own" name, which makes the car a nuisance on the highway; or in Germany that Mrs. Andrews is herself a nuisance because she is a married woman with a job, or that she is a criminal for having failed to turn her Buick over under last week's motor-sequestration regulations. None of these legal lightings affect the meaning of these same raw facts in Minnesota or New York, but it may there take on the aspect that Miss Jones is not acting "in the course of her employment" under the Workmen's Compensation Act because efficiency experting is classed legally as executive, nor within the meaning of the rule that outfits[15] answer for their employees' actions because getting to work is her own business. The figure of "lighting" is peculiarly pertinent, indeed, because, as the illustrations show, the legally

13. [Llewellyn is referring here to state securities commissions and regulators.]

14. [A reference, not common but not unique to Llewellyn, to the changing color of the sky as the sun heads westward.]

15. ["Outfits" meaning "companies" or "businesses" in this context.]

significant not merely picks particular phases *out of* the situation, but carries something *into* that situation which is not there by nature: it puts a *contract* into the situation, it thrusts in other people who are or who have been or may be in *legally* similar situations, so that Miss Jones and her job and her Buick and the highway are swept along into some *type*, which they were not at all, before the legal order went to work on them. And a layman who saw Miss Jones driving might, *or might not*, see the occurrence as having a significance resembling that which the lawman finds in it or puts into it.

And there begins a trouble. If laymen, or more accurately, if the relatively few of the heterogeneous multitude of laymen who happen to be pertinent to a type of situation do size up the type roughly as the lawmen do, and size up the lines of significance roughly as the lawmen do, then the order of society and the order of the technical world of rules of law play ball together, and writers who may take "the legal order" as pretty well covering both together are using a vocabulary accurate enough for any legal purpose. If, on the other hand, the relevant laymen and the lawmen either mark out their types differently or work in terms of divergent or cross-purposing lines of significance in the situation, then the order of society and the technical legal order tangle. So much of the lawman as is still a layman responds to the context and urge of the social order; so much of the judge, even as lawman, as is sensitive to the urge for rough justice as a proper outcome of adjudication, responds again to the context of the social order; but so much of the lawman as is pure and proud technician, and so much especially of the judge as feels *bound* to and by the articulate rules and reasoning of the craft, pulls in the direction of the technical legal order.

I pause to remind that the positive legal meaning of a positive rule of law is found in the active meaning which the authoritative organs of the State-machine do give the rule in their action.[16] Any other meaning may be in true accord with past precedent, or with accepted and revered tradition, or with what ought to be recognized as basic principle, or with the clear language of the rule or with ethical decency or with horse-sense or with Divine command; but what any other meaning is *not*, is positive [law] and authoritatively backed by State sanction. When the authoritative judges go

16. [The sentence in the text closely resembles two of the iconic quotations of the Realist perspective on rules: "We are under a Constitution, but the Constitution is what the judges say it is," by Charles Evans Hughes, *Speech Before the Elmira Chamber of Commerce* (1907), in *Addresses of Charles Evans Hughes, 1906–1916*, at 185 (2d ed, Putnam 1916); "[W]hoever hath an absolute authority to interpret and written or spoken laws, it is he who is truly the Law Giver," by Bishop Benjamin Hoadly of Bangor (1717), as quoted in John Chipman Gray, *The Nature and Sources of Law* 102 (Putnam 1909).]

"wrong", the positive rule of law goes wrong with them, and stays wrong so long as they do. We always recognize this ten years later. We always, and very properly, refuse to recognize it at the moment. Our ideals of and for the positive rule of law are live in us, and our best pressure on the judges for tomorrow is to show, today by each today, our dissatisfaction with their [ ] "wrongness" of yesterday. Our ideals then challenge the judges' power of positivity in language which denies the patent fact that the power is theirs, in order that we may press upon the *manner* of use of their power. Which is very proper, and which has its measure of effect; but the language used is not the language of dispassionate observation; it is a technique of argument and expression of emotion. Dispassionate perception comes rather from those of the bar who are *not* interested in the cause or in the question; they simply note that the rule now is what by the action of the court it has become.

This recurring point duly recalled, we come to the effects of contextual cross-pull on the rules. The effect both most frequent and most bothersome is to unsettle the rules of law. The ways of the process are plain. The court can set itself in the strictly legal order, and more particularly in the opposite more explicit phases of that order, look in strai[gh]t legal terms for the legally significant and let responsibility for any outrage rest upon "the law". This, when we find it, we know as legalism. It is frequent enough: It expresses *one* of the judges' duties, which is to abide by the rules of law. It may at times involve and evoke craftsmanship so expert and so delicate as to stir the pulse; it still is the work of legal measures and legal personnel whose ritual has lost touch for the moment with its dominant purpose, and which thus builds further into isolation instead of building toward reintegration of the rule and what the rule is for. The second, and rarer, thing the court can do is a creative job of somewhat reshaping the rule to make the legally significant explicitly approach nearer to the sanely significant, as the latter is indicated by the going order of society in what are conceived to be its more desirable phases. This calls for insight, for conviction, and for some craftsmanship; and it calls for time enough to use all three; it is, in consequence, the least frequent of the three courses which are open. Its likelihood of occurrence increases somewhat with persistence of a discrepancy between the technical order and the order of society, and in measure as repeated failures to turn to it come to pile up confusion and bafflement, and so to press judges or writers or both to direct the needed qualities upon the particular problem-situation. But be it noted that even the prophetic reformulation which has in it resolution and release does not work resolution and release save within the given jurisdictional ambit of the court which speaks. The solving rule has still to *win acceptance*. The third and perhaps most frequent course is to stall, consciously and unconsciously, and to work out a decent solution of the cause in hand (following the fall of social order significance) without risking any alteration in the explicit rules. The ways of doing this are too many to list; a few will serve for illustration. One can seize on a minor technical error, to reverse, or can ignore a major one, to affirm, as the cause requires. One can "interpret" "the" facts until they are fitted to some thoroughly accepted rule which brings the just result in the cause. One can fudge logic, in a loose opinion. One can ignore the loser's main and verbally embarrassing point. One can confuse the issue and then just bull through to a conclusion. Such are the cruder devices. More delicate ones work, for instance, by selective dialectic: take one cleanly vulnerable case as typical of a whole argument, and demolish the applicability or authority of that case—and the like. All such procedures are likely to make up in soundness of feeling for the cause what they lack in frankness or clarity in the writing. They save a court work and worry in thinking possible modification through, they give it a second or a third chance, with increased information, to think the situation over. They save it from artificial distinctions which will rise to plague it later. But they have two costs. First, they cost in clarity and certainty of result—and so of rule. That cost is ostriched at, it is not removed. Second, they cost indirectly, in lowering the standard of clarity and frankness to which the highest authority holds itself, and so is held. "John Doe at times", writes [Roscoe] Pound, "must suffer for the commonwealth". And that is true. Good rules for most cannot give custom-fit to every person, however appealing may be his particular case. But by the same token, the commonwealth also suffers, on the side of legal clarity, for poor John Doe.

CHAPTER VI

Our Situational Concepts

We gain much for clarity of discussion by fixing on propositional form as an ideal for statement of a rule of law. We can gain as much more if we select a single form of proposition, a standard scheme of proposition, as representing the ideal. For if that be feasible, we shall have a way of narrowing the points of variation, and of so setting out any rule under consideration that any variations in it may be forced to our attention. Happily enough, despite the huge variety of form which current rules of law have, any of them is reducible to statement in as simple a scheme as 2+2=4. For the variable elements in a propositional rule of law are two, and two only. The *sphere of application* can vary, the *legal consequence* can vary. There is nothing else left to vary. Hence the scheme, for any nice statement and nice analysis is as simple as

If *x*, then *y*.

X, the first variable concept, is a category or class of possible state[s] of fact (as: "Dealers selling wares which contain a hidden defect through which a buyer suffers personal injury"). *Y*, the second variable, is a category or class of legal consequence ordained by the positive authority concerned to *follow* on due official perception that a state of fact duly presented for official action falls within the category *x* (as: "are to be made to pay damages to an injured buyer in the amount of the injury.") The assumptions as to the nature of the categories are constant. What varies is either the sphere of application of the rule or the ordained legal consequence, or both, and nothing more. Moreover, since the number of types of legal consequence which are current in our system is not too great (however important the nature and clarity and effectiveness of the legal consequence is to the individual or group concerned) it is apparent that the scheme invites peculiar attention to the variable *x*, the sphere of a rule's application. And of course for purposes of guiding action, it is *x* which is the heart of the inquiry. To get guidance *from the rule of law* means in first instance that we have certainty and we hope even ease in telling what states of actual fact "are" *x*, and what states are not.

The advantages of thus reducing our ideal scheme to its baldest form is to reveal something about the nature of rules of law in their technical form: it reveals that *any* variation in *x* means a variation in the rule; any indefiniteness in a "positive" *x* means an indefiniteness in a positive rule. Our attention focusses on the variable. We see that two concepts: that of the particular sphere of application and that of the particular legal consequence, give the rule its entire body, its entire juice, its entire distinctive meaning. And this is a notable help in further discussion, because it frees us from a confusion very easy to run into: one between "rules of law" and "legal concepts". When we discuss either, we discuss the other. Any variation in either means to that precise extent a variation in the other. If we can remember that, much underbrush will be cleared out of this patch of woods.

We must not, however, get swept by words into word-jugglery. Writers who set up "legal concepts" along "rules of law" as two of the constituent materials of our "law" are not using "concepts" quite as we are; and they are not indulging in mere duplication of the same idea. By "rules" they are likely to be meaning pretty much what we do. But by "legal concepts," they mean not merely our *x* or our *y*, our described sphere of application or described legal consequence, but some major or minor classification found in our going system which ties together in a sort of organized and almost living whole a whole tribe of related rules of law: "sale" (of goods); "contract"; "trust"; "public utility"; "due process of law"; "clean hands"; "larceny" (not "theft," which is a lay idea); "corporation" (not Gesellschaft mit beschränkter H[a]ftung,[1] nor the English "limited company"); "cause of action"; "chose in action"—these last being weird technical monsters baffling to describe, but with vitality. Such "legal concepts" can, in a rough sketch, be contrasted well with mere single rules; but we shall do well to remember what we observed in Chapter IV, to wit, that such are the categories *given* us by the technical legal order as the proper units *to have rules of law about*. Which is to say, such of them as have fact-implications fit into our "If *x*, then *y*" scheme quite satisfactorily; it is only that there will be a hundred different legal

1. [Literally, "company with limited liability." The manuscript uses the word "Hoftung," but whether this was a typographical error (likely) or Llewellyn's mistaken German (highly unlikely) is not entirely clear. Nevertheless, the proper word is "Haftung."]

consequences [that] will, in one complex rule a book long or in a hundred separate rules, [ ] serve as *y*. So with "sale" or "trust" or "public utility." If on the other hand the concepts are of the legal consequence side: "injunction"; "execution"—then they will turn up in their thousands of rules with variant spheres of application.

So much we need to note, for clarity's sake. But we have not with that exhausted the meaning of these "legal concepts" which some set side by side with "rules" as members of equal rank among our "law's" constituent materials. If ours were a systematic and ordered body of law-stuff, distilled through the retorts[2] of generations of trained *jurists*, instead of being what it is, an unsystematic going system built by accretion plus *occasional* effort at conscious organization on the part not of jurists, but of practical-minded lawyers and judges and legislators—if, I say, our law-stuff were systematic and juristically sterilized, then all the "legal concepts" on hand could be handled in comfort by our pretty schematization. For in such a body of law every concept is either defined as to sphere of application, or is defined as to the kind and scope of legal consequence it describes, or both. We should have only to take cognizance of the aspect I had in mind when I spoke of these concepts as "almost living," their power of growth, their drive for development, which perceptibly, in many cases, runs along some lines and resists movement along others. And that, as I hope to show in Chapter VIII, is not too hard to take due account of. But our legal system is not thus juristified. And it therefore contains concepts which stand with one foot in fact and one foot in legal consequence, and, in addition, are often enough defined on *neither* end. Thus "public utility" is a concept which with some clarity includes a railroad and a power company, but nobody know[s] quite what else; and it includes the idea of a goodly body of legal consequences, such as considerable regulation by government, but exactly what or how much regulation is moderately indefinite. Our law is full of such concepts, and when they appear in their straddle-aspect, ranging into the worlds of fact and legal consequence both at once, they do not fit our simple propositional scheme. They represent another place where no logical formulation can catch the going essence without mutilation. Let it be stated plainly, then, that "concept" in this book is used in its sense in logic, an[d] means *any* concept; and that "legal concept" is used in our discussion as referring to one of the terms in our simplified scheme of rule. When we have need of referring further to these amphibians of our legal system, in their aspect of living in two worlds of law and fact, we shall give them a distinctive

2. ["Retort" is used here to refer to the glass container that is part of a distilling apparatus.]

label—say straddle-concepts. And since the "situational concepts" to which I shall shortly come are frequently straddle-concepts as well, let me further state plainly that in this chapter they are to be examined on the side *only* of their sphere of application.

With this out of the way, there is yet left one difficulty with our scheme of propositional rules of law. A skeptical lawman will note at once that we have for instance one rule to the effect that persons under age are not held fully to their engagements, and another that bargain-agreements for future exchange of performance obligate both parties, and another, in many states, that business agreements made on Sunday get no enforcement from the courts and another that the powers of agents are limited to what they have been instructed to do, or at least do what the principal is responsible for their being reasonably thought authorized to do. And he will urge that where a seventeen-year-old agrees on a Sunday to buy a car on installments from an auto salesman, and receives, drives and smashes the car, it is a little silly to set up one x to cover this case with an appropriate y, when the usual procedure is to play with the familiar rules, with their familiar connotations of history and policy, one upon the other until we find our way out. It is these somewhat broader and more abstract rules, our skeptic will urge properly, which we need; if rules were framed on cases like the case put, they would be unclassifiable chaos. Which is right enough, but does not touch our point. We care not how broad or how narrow, how ultra-abstract or almost concrete be our x. We need a scheme which will cover *any* rule of law; and our skeptic will agree that the legal "infant's" case has under our system to be decided as all like cases would be—which means that it makes a rule.[3] It is not one of much significance. There our skeptic makes a point. Indeed, most of the time it will not pay us to resolve rules we discuss into the concededly artificial scheme-form set forth. But where nice thinking becomes needed, then it will pay. The threat of the scheme-form in the background, to force us into nice statement, may be hoped to keep our phrasing and thinking more exact even when the form is not used. And it does make it possible to remember easily that when a concept varies by but a hair, so does the rule of law. It does force and whip into attention that the problem of guidance by rules is the problem of guiding, by rules of law, the classification of emergent raw states of fact; that the problem of control by

3. [On the way in which rules, by virtue of their generality, determine which cases are alike, and thus on the way in which the mandate to "decide like cases alike" is simply a restatement of the idea of a rule, see H.L.A. Hart, *Positivism and the Separation of Law and Morals*, 71 Harv L Rev 593, 623–24 (1958). And see also Frederick Schauer, *Profiles, Probabilities, and Stereotypes* 199–207 (Harvard 2003).]

rules means that of bringing personnel of differing personality, intelligence, background, and desire to classify with results significantly similar. [ ][4]

By "situational concept" I mean a concept indicated by a word or phrase which a layman would recognize without definition, and whose application a layman would undertake, out of the experience of his own life and without feeling an anticipatory need for definition or for technical instruction. When such a word or phrase is used to indicate and describe the area of application of a rule of law, we have a situational legal concept. Note that I do not say: "when such a word or phrase is used to *define* the area of application." Definition calls for precise thought, at least for effort at precise thought, in advance. Definition is fencing out as well as fencing in, it is *ex*clusion as well as *in*clusion, in advance; it is a conscious effort, in advance, to fix sharp edges of the concept with finality. Whereas a situational concept begins with a core and not with a boundary, begins with common sense obviousness which does not seem to need definition, begins with what anybody of sense can *recognize*, and lets it go at that. It describes, it indicates; it does not define. There is no more striking characteristic of our legal system than its tendency to go to bat in this manner; nor has our legal system ever come upon a tool of lovelier possibility. It is a technical, and verbal, device for giving almost self-operating satisfaction to the need for constant infusion into the technical structure of osmotic feeding from the social order; it is a technical, verbal device for getting that need filled imperceptibly, effectively, without men's having to *think* about the need.

The difficulty is that it will not make friends with that other tendency which is also powerful in our legal system, the drive for conforming our rules of law and our work with them—our "legal thinking"—to the dictates of a logic conceived as expressing not only the laws of valid inference, but also the existential truth about the world of rules of law *and* of the social

4. [At this point Llewellyn then wrote "Our thesis is" and stopped there. The manuscript, which had in this chapter up to this point numbered the pages in the form of "Rules VI (4)," then picks up with a page numbered "Rules VI—12." Because a compilation in Llewellyn's own hand describes Chapter VI as encompassing pages "1–6, 12–28," and because William Twining's 1964 compilation initially describes Chapter VI as containing 28 pages but then crosses this out and substitutes "23 pp.," the most plausible inference is that Llewellyn abruptly stopped work on the first version of the chapter mid-sentence on page 6, started anew on the entire chapter at some subsequent time, and ultimately, having decided to use the first version of the beginning of the chapter rather than the rewritten one, simply discarded the first 11 pages of the rewritten version.]

order. For any logic calls for definitions, early and clear, and calls for rigor in their use.

It needs little discussion that the great classifications of our technical legal order began in the main with such situational concepts of what was significantly there as a set of units to make rules of law about. The "relational" thinking of the common law world on which [Roscoe] Pound properly puts stress[5] goes back to situations seen thus as obviously significant to any man: "baron et feme," with its later and democratized "husband and wife"; "master and servant"; "landlord and tenant"; "vendor and purchaser" (of land); "principal and agent"; "guardian and ward." The double name is not essential: "trust" meant what it says in plain lay terms free equally of association with the rules of the chancellor and of association with fat persons with large cigars and dollar signs on their hats.[6] "Sale" was a plain type of transaction. "Slander" was slander, "carriers" was a lay and not a legal term, "wills" were wills, and "bills of exchange" had not yet become part of "negotiable instruments" but were just merchants' standard devices for getting credits from one center to another. The same holds of lesser concepts within the greater, domicile and support in the husband and wife situation; wage, custody, fidelity in that of master and servant; the res of the trust, the trustee's duty to account; the carrier's receipt, or "common" character; the indorser on the maturity of a bill of exchange. Nor need we go back into ancient history to find such turning to situational concepts. The 19th Century built up a body of rules on Offer and Acceptance, or on Third Party Beneficiaries of contracts, as surely on a foundation of situational concept as the 17th Century had built its body of rules on Accord and Satisfaction. The 20th has made a body of rules on "letters of credit," picking the concept out of current commerce in the teeth of what the law books had to say about the term. "Labor" emerges from lay speech, not law speech, as the name integrating a new field of law around the factory, with "strike," "lockout," "boycott," "picketing," figuring as concepts beside "injunction."

Now of situational concepts several things need saying. First: they are never hit upon, save because the situation is seen as significant for legal purposes. In the beginning the very name of the situation carries a flavor, and a strong flavor, of the reason for seeing that situation as significant. Common sense identification of the new state of fact with the type, or exclusion of it

5. [See Roscoe Pound, *The Spirit of the Common Law* 12–29 (Marshall Jones 1921); Roscoe Pound, *The End of Law as Developed in Juristic Thought II: The Nineteenth Century*, 30 Harv L Rev 201, 212–16 (1917).]

6. [The latter reference is to large monopolizing businesses, a usage that generated the term "antitrust."]

from the type, will be guided by the implicit sense of that significance of the situation even where badly described—for a time; for a layman or a judge to see is for him to recognize, provided only the state of fact seen, however novel, be "*well* within" the flavor of the classification: provided only it be within the *core* of the sense. This is the situational concept in its period of glory: open-ended, flexible, ready of application, infusing any minor change of fact unnoticed into the law, keeping the rules of positive law thus without intellectual effort abreast of movement in conditions.

The second thing is that no clarity of core, however radiant, suffices to mark boundaries, in *close* cases, for *general* agreement. That is a job for specialists, for specialists with authority to select and settle among conflicting claims. It is a job for intellectual techniques, it is a job for sophisticated procedures. And the nature of law-stuff, whether seen as centering on dispute or seen as centering on regulation or seen as centering on both, is that it must deal with men and groupings of men who are straining to get or to use or to gouge out or to expand into or to defend *all* that the going legal system will yield them as against their competitors or their adversaries or the general elbow-room of the vicinity. Bad men, greedy men, exuberant men, ambitious men, excited men, men in combat, seek to turn leeway their way. So that close cases, even in a relatively stable culture, have a habit of turning up; and in a mobile culture they pop up frequently. When the close case becomes a matter for the technician, the situational concept becomes a subject of conscious puzzlement. It has to. It becomes the subject of conscious ruling. It has to. It becomes the object of precedent-making, in the well known process of successive inclusions and exclusions which prick out its border more precisely than ordinary men have need or desire to prick it out. I need not emphasize that this need not yet mean *definition*, especially not the casting of final definition into words; thither the series of successive close cases presses, but it may be long before the definition is achieved. What I do need to emphasize is that the technical authoritative record, for technicians' use, of when we have the relevant situation and when we do not have it, begins to accumulate as material, each part of which is fixed in the record as of its time and circumstances of incidence, no longer moving unnoticed with those lesser changes of circumstance within the social order which *shift the core* of a situational concept, for the layman, with none but an aging grandfather becoming articulate in words or thought about the shift. Sooner or later, if the states of fact shift their significance or their lines of significance for laymen, there must then come tension or strain between the situational concept as it becomes formalized in the legal order, and as its material for "application" is found outside.

The third thing has to do with both the nature and the labelling of a situational concept. Concepts are indeed always chosen (or grow) with an eye to some significance, but sometimes lines of significance which originally coincided come later into tangle. This is perhaps peculiarly true of situational concepts. For a situational concept has to do with some collection of events or people or both seen as recurring, seen as a type. The name or label we give it designates that collocation, and only by luck will that name or label also include a reminder of *why* we picked out the collocation of people or events or both to notice *as* a type worth putting a label on. We have, for instance, a situational concept of "account stated," with rules of law clustered around it which give it a peculiarly definitive character in settling up the state of obligation. It was built around periodic reckoning up of running accounts in a world in which book-keeping was not yet what it now is, prices for goods shipped were not reckoned by contract in advance, currencies varied from town to town, and mails were slow. "Stated" had then a punch. It implied thoughtful, careful going over on both sides as for a grave affair, and it implied real need for getting clarity about a fresh start. None of this is in the flavor of the label as the conditions on which the high significance of the situation rested have moved from under. The principle has faded out.

A more pervasive and instructive instance may be the debt-and-mortgage concept. Thus the use by a farmer of his farm as security for a loan, while he continues to hold and work the farm, has struck us as significant, and we have given such a collocation of events the name of "mortgaging," and the resulting situation we have labelled "mortgage." Two features stand out which the name does nothing to remind us of. One is that no lender in his senses lends on a farm without an eye on the farmer; and that American farmers as distinct from many European peasants are likely not to have a tradition of three hundred years in the same father-to-son succession which makes loss of a given farm a loss of root, caste, family honor; loss of the American farmer's farm is more likely to be the failure of an individual enterpriser in an enterprise not too much unlike the wiping out of an enterpriser's hopes and capital in failure of a shop. There is then reason for seeing the pressure of personal obligation, of the debt, as an inherent part of this "mortgage" situation. But in the development of city real estate under the influence of limited liability for corporate investment we find this same mortgage concept carried over to a corporation known as 130 Locust St. Inc., whose total assets consist of what is found at 130 Locus St. *Personal* obligation in any meaningful sense there is none; but the "situation" is seen as still requiring the presence, in the collocation, of a "personal" obligation;

the "corporation" signs a note or bond as well as a mortgage-paper. This is mere waste. But when city lenders, now accustomed to lending "on the realty," not on the man-and-the-realty, decide that Jo Salvatore's home will not stand a loan, this same seeing of "the" situation, if he and his lenders guess wrong about the lines of the city's growth, will cost him his savings and his life insurance and his fruit store—these go to satisfy the "deficiency" judgment on his personal obligation, though these had not been figured into the lender's bargain. Still less does the lender initially figure on getting a "personal" claim against O'Reilly, if he buys from Salvatore; nor does O'Reilly, who buys knowing "there is a mortgage of $3000 on it," figuring that he is risking *his* savings, life insurance and garage business, over and above "what he puts into the house" and his psychic investment in a real home of his own. But the situational concept "mortgage" has typified itself upon an ancient model, and has found legal form and structure to keep the type pure upon the ancient purpose of it: a mortgage is "an incident to a debt": there "can be no mortgage without a debt"; we must create a pseudo-debt of 130 Locus St., Inc., to "sustain" the security-interest in 130 Locust St. which is what we are interested in; and Salvatore and O'Reilly suffer as by the hand of fate. It is obvious that as a matter of intelligent arrangement of modern affairs there is no point in this. It is obvious that real estate "lending" and "borrowing" would proceed more adequately if there were two devices: the security-interest alone, akin to a pawn; and the security-interest with the personal obligation of a true borrower added, when that obligation is needed, to help assure sound management and care of the realty. Such a division of possible devices makes for clearer meditation on both sides of the bargain, makes for clearer understanding, makes for tailoring the device and the rate of return to the risk intended. The reduction in rate to Mr. Salvatore, for instance, gained by adding his personal obligation, would rarely induce him to add it. But what interests us here is that this is, for the American legal system, discussion in the clouds. Because the *situation* which has been caught into the legal concept is "*debt-and-*mortgage," so that "mortgage" implies a "debt." What interests us further is, first, that there was once, and in many instances is still, a reason for seeing this whole collocation as a unit; second, that the reason is not explicit, but only implicit, in the labelling of the concept; third, that "the" situation as envisaged by and caught into the concept absorbs without hesitation, worry, or heavy intellectualization such later situations as the 130 Locust St. deal, or even the corporate serial issue of bonds bottomed on an intricate mortgaging, and also the development of the subdivision in which Salvatore thought to find a permanent home; fourth, and finally, that that automatic absorption goes on including new situations without reference to whether they still fit the implicit reason for originally fixing on "the" situation as a significant type; and that there can be automatic exclusion *and so invalidation* of other situations which have by later turn of fact become significantly similar.

In this "mortgage" field we can see the situational concept perhaps at its maximum utility, certainly at its maximum effectiveness. Movement of underlying fact pattern has been relatively slow, which makes absorption vastly easier and vastly more certain. For changes of fact-pattern of action which occur slowly are changes which we notice almost not at all, and with which our minds like our bodies just move along. "Patterns" is indeed an artificial word for rough indication of instances of behavior which if accurately described would be charted not as a line, but as a scattering belt, with various instances out toward the edges being seen as queer, or as rather interesting deviations, or even as objectionable variants. Such a belt of behavior moves, and we notice little—save that after fifty years, or twenty, we look back and remember that it wasn't like this when we were young. But we cannot say *when* "the" change came—the new variants in behavior just slid in: "people were beginning to . . ."; in our mortgage field the last war "brought in" baby bonds without mortgages, but mortgages "came to" be added; and city realty bonds "came in"; and subdivision development meandered through its multiple and sometimes devious channels. The situational concept on hand kept up.

It kept up, better than it can be counted on to keep up throughout the field of law, because real estate is an area of operation in which two factors operate to a degree non-typical of our field of law at large. The first is, as has already been mentioned, that the rules of law in that area tend to be tighter in both verbal and conceptual formulation than our rules of law in general. Which might seem for a moment to tell *against* the concepts keeping up with change, were it not for the second factor: that real estate, and real estate security especially, are areas in which the law-consumer, to an altogether peculiar degree, has learned to call in a lawyer, and to let the lawyer shape the transaction. Thus over the years each novel raw situation as it emerged out of the social order was worked over by lawmen to *fit* the situational concept prevailing in the legal order, and reached the judges in a form whose ready classification was furthered not only by normal insight but by anticipatory art. This, plainly, will produce more in the way of clarity, certainty, and keeping up than situational concepts can be hoped to yield where the lawyer's shaping hand is not put to the clay of life while the clay is still soft. And even under these favoring conditions, we have seen that our concept can slip into blindish and troubling misfit. What the peculiar conditions prevailing in this area at once of real estate law and of security give us is not only some reduction of the quantum of misfit, but, and above all, a degree of certainty that, given a strain of the technical legal order will, *here*, prevail. A decision which outrages lay common sense and decency can, in *such* a field, attain and retain a reasonable degree of predictive certainty. On the other hand, attempts at readaptation of the situational concept to reach the changing essence of some new situation achieve no such predictive certainty. Thus when the reality as it stands comes less and less to gather into itself control of the intended factual security—when, for instance, for the farm is substituted a business with fairly high turnover in proportion to fixed assets, and when first claim on going income looms larger than first claim on land and structure, and going value of an organization looms larger than any physical equipment—in such a situation the efforts of even the most skilled of counsel to lay legal hold upon the desired juice of the security remain experimental ventures, needing court-test step by step before they approach the stage of being more than, let us say, intelligent and rather well-advised gambles.

In sum, then, what we find in the situational concept is something we can show the man from Mars as a communication device which under favoring circumstances guarantees us a very fair measure of certainty in dealing with unforeseen changes in situations, irrespective of official personnel. Limitations it has, in regard to the adequacy of the adjustment. Plainly also, lacking further inquiry, we should not dare point to it as doing such good service unless we could guarantee also the prevalence of a practice of consulting a lawman before new situations were cast into final shape.

Before we venture into an area where men are just doing things, without having lawmen at their elbow, there is an observation to be made about the way in which rules of law, in our going system, get themselves set up. Our current positive rules come, to an amazing extent, in pairs; and of any pair, one half is as likely as not to be implicit, and to find no formulation in the books at all. Thus the Uniform Sales Act which has semi-codified the law on sales of goods for most of our States, lays it down that "In a sale by sample, there is an implied warranty that the bulk shall correspond with the sample." It may seem finical overexactitude to point out that this implies a negative twin rule: "In anything which is not a sale [by] sample, there is no implied warranty that the bulk shall correspond with the sample"—a rule which I do not remember eve[r] to have seen expressed; but some such rule is implicit and present for use; and any case which turns on *whether* there was a sale by sample will, if the facts be found to contain none, refuse the buyer any damages he may be claiming because the bulk did not comply with the sample.[7] Such negative twin rules derive rarely from explicit language: they derive from context. The context may be a context of common sense, or it may be a technical context, but whether it be the one or the other or a mixture of the two, if it is a context, it is implicit. And *if* implicit, it runs danger of ambiguity or multiguity. This is not an idle observation. Such ambiguities and multiguities make litigation, make uncertainty. Thus, for instance, a similar rule of Sales law attaches to the selling of food an obligation (an "implied warranty") that it shall be fit for human consumption; but the outlines of the implicit negative twin rule have been drawn into question. It has been made the subject of repeated litigation, with courts divided about the answer, whether if food—ice-cream, say—was not *sold* to be taken away, but was *served* to be eaten on the premises, obligation on the server was thereby negated.

Morris[8] has pointed out what is certainly a lively, though not an exclusive, tendency in our legal system: a tendency among the lawmen to assume that the area of conceivable, and so of problematical, applicability of a rule of law has been *exhaustively* classified by the current rules: "Sale by sample" carries the obligation on the seller that the bulk shall correspond, *and nothing else* which might conceivably do so, does. Sometimes the classification is not only exhaustive, but is explicitly so, and the competing situations have received each a name of its own. This represents a material technical advance, for multiguity is out; every problem situation has to be thrown one way or the other. And there is a further possible technical advance: for a pair of contrasting labels can give sure guidance much more easily than can a single label. If, for instance, what we are after is to spot the kind of promissory proposal of a deal which, if agreed to, becomes that legally binding obligation we call "contract," then we can make out with the situational concept "Offer" to describe it. But it is tough going to be wrestling with "whether this offer is a legal Offer or is a Not-Offer"; we sharpen our problem if we label the companion category and then label the problem-category as well, and inquire "whether this proposal is a mere preliminary negotiation or is a definitive offer capable of legally effective acceptance.

This last phrasing is not current, though the idea behind it is. The phrasing is an elaboration of the current phrasing, which latter indicates the two categories merely as "Offer" and "preliminary Negotiation." The difference

7. [It is not clear that Llewellyn is saying anything here not captured by the venerable maxim of *expressio unius est alterio exclusus*.]

8. [Probably legal historian Richard Morris, whose *Studies in American Legal History* was the subject of a harsh review by Llewellyn at 31 Colum L Rev 729 (1931).]

between the shorter and the more elaborate phrasing lies for our purposes in the degree to which the *reason* of the discrimination is articulated, in the degree to which the different *labellings* of the same situational concepts convey their principle. The difference suggests a fact: the fact that fortunate or skilful labelling, or skilful relabelling of what has previously travelled under unfortunate labelling, can [en]liven certainty in the application of a situational concept, and can also aid its adaptation to the unforeseen problem situation. And the fact leads to an observation which is quaint.

For it is plain that the virtue of a situational concept, its clarity, its immediacy, its freedom from need of definition, its power of expansion without conscious effort—it is plain that all of these root in the incorporation into a technical instrument, into a rule of law, of lay-stuff, untechnicized. Such incorporation, when just done, when not done of conscious purpose, is legal technique of a primitive and unsophisticated order. It is a phase of technique which harks back to a day and condition when technical law-stuff had not yet specialized out of the general matrix of what was what and what was right. It is my own belief that the retention by our law-folk and our legal system of a heavy portion of this primitive style of legal technique is a major source of the value of that legal system to us. Our feeling for the core of a broad generalization; our watching for the sense-beyond-the-exact-language of a narrow one; our reading of argument with reference to the issue, with less attention on other possibilities the sweeping words may hold; our judges' continued drive to somehow work rough justice as the end-result of an adjudication—all these are parts of the same earthy primitivity. It carries with it its defects, and they are many, and not least among them is a portion of confusion. But its major virtues: clarity in guidance for dealing with the uncharted, and constant urging of the technical legal order into rapprochement with the greater social order upon which the technical legal order plays—these are things without price. The suggestion which I may here anticipate is that the first major level of sophistication of technique in our law: that of reducing matters to fixed rules of law[,] and being bound by those rules, is at war with our healthy primitivity *only insofar as the rules are infected with rule-of-thumbishness*. The rule of thumb style of rule of law is itself a relatively primitive technique—also one, as we have seen, with its values. It is less primitive than is non-differentiation of technical matters from the general social matrix; but as an intellectual device it fails of adequacy by overdoing its correction. The evil of too much fluidity it corrects, but the correction is by substituting rigidity. Whereas a system of law needs neither fluidity nor rigidity alone, but due degree of both, in healthy interaction. The sophisticated technical device which serves both needs at once is the rule of law, as narrow or as broad as circumstances may variantly indicate, built if not on the line of explicit principle, then at least with its concepts carefully so labelled as to keep the reasons for their framing live. And a situational concept, so chosen and so labelled, can in any area where men have to deal with matters of legal import but have not the means or the habit of keeping lawmen at their elbow achieve the best that men's techniques of law and language have yet had to offer.

There is for instance in our Uniform Sales Act, as has been mentioned, no definition of the sphere of application of the rules on "sale or contract to sell by sample." "By sample" serves as an indicator. It has indicated very satisfactorily. There are much more important rules in that same Act on "sale" and "contract to sell" and "goods bought" "by description" which serve their purpose and serve it well, with no slightest effort made in the rules to define the states of fact which fall within the rules. On the other hand there are rules whose area of application is similarly just indicated by label—those on "sale or return" and "sale on approval"—which do not serve so well; this is inter alia because there has become prevalent in some trades a practice among laymen of "shipping and memorandum," the wares being delivered to the buyer and charged against him, with some understanding that he may return them, but with no clear indication in the situation of whether it falls under "sale or return" or "sale on approval" or that "mere consignment" which lawyers reckon as no sale at all.

Again, the basic concept of the whole law of agency is "authority," and the basic distinction taken upon that concept is that between "real authority" and "apparent authority." Here are situational concepts almost as clean today as they were in the beginning; and while there is analytical improvement in substituting for "authority" the concept of an agent's "powers," it is an analytical improvement which calls for conscious and sustained attention to *why* those powers exist, lest accurate statement and analysis lose its rooting in the soil of life.

One finds the Supreme Court, in reading a clause on customs duties, classing "tomato" as a vegetable in the housewife's understanding,[9] not as a fruit in the botanist's; one finds Holmes throwing to the jury the question whether a given chancy operation was a "lottery" within the meaning of a criminal statute;[10] one finds Scrutton discarding the technical niceties of the rules of Sales and reading a market statute to forbid what any dealer on the

9. [*Nix v. Hedden*, 149 US 304 (1893).]
10. [*Commonwealth v. Wright*, 137 Mass. 250 (1884).]

market would understand as "selling."[11] If these be instances of nothing more than horse-sense speaking through personnel of exalted position or reputation, the fact that horse-sense is what they are will make the point: the well-framed and well-labelled situational concept guides judge and laymen both and both together—the layman although he have no lawyer at his elbow; the judge, despite the lawyer there.

There are areas, patently, in which such guidance is not possible: the situation-concepts needed are not distinct enough, even at the core, to the relevant laymen; or too much of what is going on goes on in the less certain penumbral areas; or transactions are of lasting character and need to be built on technical rock against the unforeseen. The last of these calls for intervention of skilled counsel at the outset. The others are not the areas in which certainty is a boast our law makes good.

11. [*Ronaasen & Son v. Arcos, Ltd.*, 43 Ll L Rep 1, 5 (1932) (CA), discussed in Karl N. Llewellyn, *On Warranty of Quality and Society*, 36 Colum L Rev 699, 707 (1936). Llewellyn's admiration of Scrutton is noted in James J. White, *Good Faith and the Cooperative Antagonist*, 54 SMU L Rev 679 (2001).]

CHAPTER VII

The Advocate's Leeway

We have noted, in Chapter IV, a difference between advocate and judge in their approach to rules of law. We noted that the judge has as his office to seek guidance in such rules. Not clients' interest nor his personal desire, but health (as he feels it) of our legal scheme of things and justice (as he feels it) in outcome of the adjudication in hand, are the factors which entitle him to bear a bit to port or starboard on the tiller; in the main, the course is set by the given rules if they speak clearly enough to set a course or even indicate one. To the advocate, the rules speak a different language. His eye is on his client's interest and desire, *once he has decided to take his client's case.* His eye, *once he has embraced the cause,* is on manipulating the machinery of the rules for what that machinery can be made to yield. If the tone of the rules or their seeming or their implicit purpose is against him, his object is to hold down to their very letter the rules' effect upon the technical institutional structure, *for this cause*. If their letter tells against him, his object is to marshal every leeway the going system offers, to escape the letter by use of principle and purpose, by the reason of the matter. An advocate, once the cause is his, has as his trade to exploit not necessarily the leeway of the rules of law—for his cause may require him to seek to hold the rules within most brittle limits—but the uttermost leeway of the available lines of respectable, honorable, persuasive *argument* afforded by our going legal order. The client's right under our going scheme of things includes the right to have the system's leeway thus exploited in his favor.

That is the first point. The second is that authoritative determination waits upon advocacy, is sought by advocacy, follows only advocacy by both sides. If authoritative determination is not also *influenced* by advocacy, then all law-consumers who hire advocates have been misled, as have all advocates who ever thought they saw a way to win "a desperate case" or who in any cause at all have thought their skill worth pay. But the conclusion from this is embarrassing. For the conclusion is that if the authoritative determination is influenced by advocacy, then unless skill in advocacy is hair-balanced cause by cause between the sides, the rules of law in outcome, in meaning, in authoritative settlement of meaning, are subject to a factor of uncertainty which no man by looking at the rules alone, or even at the rules against the background of the legal order, or even at the rules against that background and in the light of the situation and the official personnel—which no man until he knows the relative caliber of the respective advocates who will face each other can cope with in advance. This, I say, is an embarrassing conclusion; it is unsettling to one's views about the clarity and meaningfulness of rules. Yet I see no escape from it.

It means that from the angle of *knowability* the positive prevailing rules of our law must have lurking in them an unsuspected quantum of the quality known to lawmen as being "unsettled." Indeed it may be argued with force that from one angle of importance no unknowable rule of law, nor any rule to the degree of its unknowability, *is* effectively positive. For it boots not, I remind you, that a formula of words regarded as a well-settled rule of law be certain of recitation by any court or every court, if that formula do not give positive *guidance* as to how to deal with emergent states of fact. The test of whether the formulas of words we have and accept do give positive guidance, that test is whether the mass of officials subject to the court of resort can tell in advance what the court of last resort will, when called on, determine that the lower officials should, under the rule, have done. This is not all there is to say about the matter,[1] but there is no sense in ducking away from this much of what there is to say: for instance, by substituting language which makes the ultimate court's ruling appear simply to have been "the rule" all along. Such language does indeed express excellent dogmatics for the decision of future cases; and for the guidance of officials in the future; and it is well for officials to be reminded by such language that they had better walk softly in cases of doubt because such is the language which will be used upon them if they gamble wild and gamble wrong. But

1. [One of the things "about the matter" that Llewellyn does not say involves the questions of final interpretive authority and of enforcement. In many areas of public law, but especially in constitutional law, the question whether the court of last resort is a court or instead some other branch of government is deeply contested. Compare Larry D. Kramer, *The People Themselves: Popular Constitutionalism and Judicial Review* (Oxford 2004), with Larry Alexander and Frederick Schauer, *On Extrajudicial Constitutional Interpretation,* 110 Harv L Rev 1359 (1997), with Michael Stokes Paulsen, *The Most Dangerous Branch: Executive Power to Say What the Law Is,* 83 Geo LJ 217 (1994). And even if the court of last resort is a court, it is hardly clear that official compliance with what that court says can be taken for granted.]

we need, also, language to express the situation while the officials have to act, and while they are not yet *guided*. That idea dear to many jurists that "promulgation" is an inherent feature of a rule of law has as its reason that the rule should be knowable, nay, must be knowable, if it is to guide. That reason applies fully to *effective* positivity. I do not wish to complicate the discussion unduly, but two consequences of this view are worth note here. They would be first, that a given current formulation of a rule of law can be wholly positive at the core,[2] and yet un-positive at its edges because entirely multiguous[3] there; and a huge number of our current formulations are of that character. The second consequence would be that effective positivity of a rule of law differs within the same jurisdiction and at a given moment according to the diagnostic skill of counsel studying the rule. A Root of New York or a Johnson of Philadelphia[4] may know what the Supreme Court will do (under his own advocacy, or without it) at a time when relatively few other lawmen, official or other, do know that; and the effective positive meaning of the rules of law is then not the same for Root or Johnson and for other men.[5] This is perhaps a shocking way to state a fact; but I submit the fact itself is shocking. It is shocking, that is, unless it is inevitable. But it is a fact which I believe to be partly evitable, and if so, a shocking way of stating it may be pardoned. For it is not good that rules of law current as such, our rules of law whose office is to guide, should read one way to the great Root (who will prove right) and another way to half the bar and to the relevant officials, and so mislead them—it is not good, at least, if by taking thought there is here half a cubit to be added to the law's stature. How firmly it is felt not to be good is evidenced when the bulk of the bar have gone wrong and have also acted on their guess, and the judges of an ultimate court then sometimes forego their own good judgment, and read a rule to mean what they do not think it means: communis error (sometimes!) facit ius.[6]

2. [Here again is a plain acknowledgment of the existence of a core of clear meaning and a fringe of doubt, precisely the point that H.L.A. Hart made in *The Concept of Law* (Penelope A. Bulloch and Joseph Raz, eds, 2d ed, Clarendon/Oxford 1994), and which in Chapter VII Hart accuses the Realists of failing to recognize.]

3. [A Llewellyn neologism, designed to suggest that just as an ambiguous word or rule can have either of two meanings, so can some words or rules have more than two meanings.]

4. [Elihu Root (1845–1917), perhaps now better known as a statesman and government official, was one of the premier litigators of the time, as was Philadelphian John G. Johnson (1841–1917), famous for defending companies charged with violations under the then-new Sherman Antitrust Act.]

5. [This is an interesting extension of a Holmesian focus on law as the prediction of judicial decisions, for the claim here is that the rule of law lies *in* the prediction and thus may vary according to the predictor.]

6. [Best translated as "collective error makes law."]

The question goes, then, to whether we have here only a dialectic trouble or a material one; to whether this phase of uncertainty is a mere incident puffed up by alarmist phrasing or is a pervasive and too little noticed trouble of some magnitude. And if the latter, the question goes to ways of dealing with it.

I propose to attempt to show the problem to be a substantial one by laying out the following considerations: First, the leeway available for exploitation by advocates which our going system offers is a *wide* leeway; I think, one particularly wide. Second, that it is a *hidden* leeway, which means not only that it and its exploitation are not easy to notice (so that general impressions of how important it is may be very tricky), but means also that manipulation of the leeway produces a peculiarly unpleasant kind of uncertainty: that unpredictability which results from the work of an unspotted factor of variation, which runs free of control because it runs free of study. Third, that an even matching of advocates so as to produce balance in their skill and cancel out their influence is rather less to be expected in our system than in most, so that the *net effect* of advocate's leeway is likely, with us, to be greater. I shall proceed then to examine one particular technical development whose detail may be instructive on the matter. From the whole there will be some attempt to figure practicable ways of reducing this source of uncertainty—this source of lessened effective positivity of our current rules.

I do not wish to range here too far into the sociology of dogmatics,[7] but I think it safe to lay down that no system of law can long continue which contains a large number of rules of law in the form of rules of thumb and concepts of thumb, without there developing for use upon those rules of thumb an appropriate body of techniques: of *ways* of using and reading the rules of thumb, of *ways* of looking over problematical states of fact to classify them thumb-wise. And these techniques are "correct" techniques. They are approved by authority; they are used by authority; they can be argued to authority and can enlist authority's interest when so argued; they can be urged upon a tribunal as proper to control and compel its action. Typically, the techniques find more or less adequate verbal expression as rules of proper dogmatics: rules for construction of statutes, rules about how to find the true rule of a precedent or of a set of precedents. The appropriate tech-

7. ["Dogmatics" is used here in the (continental) European sense of the formal structure of legal doctrine.]

niques for handling rules of thumb and concepts of thumb are directed at the latter, they cleave to the external mark, they limit or stamp out meaning and effect in wooden insistence on the word. "The statute is in derogation of the common law, and must be strictly construed"; which means, must be read not to extend beyond its letter. "The precedent is clear, and is binding upon this court"; which means, its reason is not to be inquired into. "Expressio unius est exclusio alterius"; which means that "rifle, shotgun, sawed-off shotgun or automatic pistol" does not include an air pistol which shoots a killing dart. "General words must be construed as *in pari materia*"; which means that "rifle, shotgun, sawed-off shotgun, automatic pistol or similar weapon" is quite capable of excluding a pistol which does not use powder or cartridge, or of excluding a silencer which does not shoot at all. "The meaning must be found within the four corners of the instrument; the language is clear; no evidence can be admitted to show a different meaning, for there is no ambiguity to be resolved." "The title and preamble are no part of the statute." And beyond such lines of general rationale, and cutting vastly deeper than such explicit lines, are the relevant ways and attitudes of work—those attitudes which when they become habitual with a judge of long career mark him for posterity: his is the tribe of Parke, that proud wooden mind of the Exchequer,[8] unsurpassed in the rule of thumb techniques, who owes his unenvied reputation to the fact that he used those techniques with equally incisive rigor when they did not fit. "Wrong side of the line: five dollars," in the traffic court. "Pigs is pigs": a pound of flesh; a pound of flesh without blood. If the fiduciary who has juggled two sets of stocks and bonds between two accounts, embezzling from both but leaving enough to meet recurring audit in either—if he is a "trustee," then the last account in which he placed the bonds he kept can keep them all, but if he is an "agent," the account he took them out of can recover them—not because of any reason in the distinction, but because the shadows of two words with different happenstance of marks lie on the picture.

On the other hand, given in the technical legal order a habit of seeing rules—*much* of the time—as having some sense not wholly or finally bounded by particular words, though indeed indicated by words; given, even with a statute whose words stand black, unchanging, on the page, a habit and attitude—*much* of the time—of looking for that statute's intent, its purpose, its wholeness, and reading its words in the light of that which is

8. [The reference is to Baron James Parke of the Court of Exchequer, who sat in the 1830s and 1840s, and whose well-known opinions included *Winterbottom v. Wright*, (1842) 152 Eng Rep 402 (Exch), and *Langridge v. Levy*, (1837) 150 Eng Rep 863 (Exch).]

not in its words; given a practice of lending readier ear to the core of meaning than to the outward ranges of its implication—then there will almost of necessity develop around these habits and techniques a different and contrasting body of rationale, a rationale for escaping any language, however authoritative and however explicit. Doubly so when a goodly body of rules of law themselves are framed—as so many of ours are—upon lines of principle; doubly so when a goodly body of concepts are and have been those direct-perception instruments which escape definitional attack: the situational concepts. These rationales for escaping language-limits will also be respectable, honorable, current. They will also be built to catch a tribunal's ear as proper to persuade, control, compel its action. "The true intention of the parties is to be determined, and the document must be examined as a whole, and in the light of the circumstances." The precedent which is so clear represents a misapplication of the true principle, if not indeed a misconception of it; the precedent can, moreover, be distinguished, and the rule there laid down was quite unnecessary to the decision. "Rifle, shotgun, sawed-off shotgun, or automatic pistol" must be read in light of the evil at which the statute is directed, and adequately covers any propulsive weapon capable of individual and deadly use, and even a separate device whose only function is to facilitate the evil in view.[9] The legislation is highly remedial; it must be liberally construed so as to effectuate its purpose. The rule, though well established, is based upon an older condition of affairs, and must be modified to fit its essential reason;[10] "it has ever been the glory of the common law that it adjusts itself to new conditions."[11]

I am not pointing out here merely what every common lawyer knows, knows in his fingers, knows in and from his daily work, to wit, that a case can hope to stand for anything it says, on the one hand, and that any judicial language, however off the point of the decision, is well worth setting forth in quotes. Whereas, on the other hand, a case can hope to be distinguished

9. [In a criminal statute, it is hardly clear that Llewellyn's approach would survive application of the rule of lenity, requiring statutory ambiguity to be resolved in favor of the defendant, and seeming to prohibit as well, a fortiori, extension of a criminal statute beyond what its words will naturally bear. For a recent discussion of the rule of lenity, see *United States v. Santos*, 128 S Ct 2020 (2008).]

10. [Insofar as Llewellyn is still referring to the *statutory* language about rifles and shotguns and the like, his eager application of common law method even to modify the literal words of a statute anticipates, for example, Guido Calabresi, *A Common Law for the Age of Statutes* (Harvard 1982).]

11. [The source of this exact quotation is obscure, but something like it was part of the common language of Llewellyn's time—and earlier. See, for example, Lee Max Friedman, *The Bicycle and the Common Carrier*, 12 Harv L Rev 119, 119 (1898).]

down to its narrowest facts and issue. And that the appropriate techniques of using cases either way, or in any of the multiform intermediate variants, are of the most familiar and respectable, and can be employed with face, grace, and propriety all in the same argument—on different prior decisions.[12] That fact deserves to be recalled here, as suggesting one line of advocates' leeway—one limited only by [Samuel] Williston's shrewd observation that once a *practice* is established in the system of seeing a given precedent or set of precedents some one way rather than in any other, thereafter that set of precedents becomes vastly less fluid; its working over tends then to have been accomplished. But that is not what I am chiefly concerned here to point out, because that is a leeway limited to the case-law side of our legal system. Whereas the distinction between rule-of-thumb technique and the technique of purpose and principle, and the leeway which that distinction beckons any advocate to exploit: these hold *throughout* our legal scheme of things. They hold for case-law, they hold for construction of contract and transaction, they hold for statute, they hold for Constitution, they hold for any combination of them all. Even within the greater normal rigidity of rules "of property" and of criminal law there are such leeways, though their range is less.

With this we come to the nub of the situation. It lies here: if the thumbish technique and rationale were limited to rules of thumb which showed cause for being treated as rules of thumb, then advocates on the two sides of a cause would be fighting with appropriate weapons over a narrow battleground. Whether or not their skill was balanced, such a contest could not help but get the issue somewhat more sharply focussed. And of our courts it may be said with powerful show of soundness that when an issue is sharply focussed and argued by both sides to the point and along lines which are comparable, there is a very fair degree of predictability of outcome. Again, if the attitudes and rationale of principle and purpose were confined to rules and concepts which showed cause for being dealt with on lines of principle and purpose, then advocates on the two sides of a cause would be opposing reason to reason. And even with skill and persuasiveness out of balance, their net work could not well avoid informing the court's thought. There is range of doubt when reason opposes reason, there is range of doubt when

12. [The importance of the previous sentences should not be overlooked. If an argument for what a court *said* is always available to one side, and if an argument distinguishing that case on its facts is always available to the other side, and if there is no requirement that one side or another be consistent about which *type* of argument it uses, then the degree of precedential indeterminacy is indeed vast.]

the applicability of a reason to a situation is in question. But there is no such vastly deep of doubt as when the gamble turns instead on whether reason will be applied at all, *any* reason, or mere rule of thumb.

Here, I say, is the nub. For when technical measures are in issue (and technical measures are in issue in every case at law) and technical results of technical measures are the subject of the controversy (and technical results of technical measures are the subject of every controversy at law) and when there is enough plausibility of doubt to admit of hearing argument,[13] then authoritative materials mixed of thumbishness and principle will yield a different specific outcome according to whether thumbishness or principle be the line of treatment by the tribunal. If, and so long as, we lack clear guidance as to *which* line the tribunal will bring to bear, we lack clear guidance as to what the outcome will be—we lack clear guidance as to what the tribunal will tell us we should have known the rule to mean.

Here is a simple instance. New York has a vigorous usury law, making loans at more than six per cent flatly non-recoverable: "void." The courts understand its policy. They have held the voidity to infect a usurious note so that even a holder in due course gets no better rights against the maker than the lender had. New York has, however, a number of exceptions from its rule on usury, which look to legitimatizing certain lines of transaction in which greater rates of interest are common and are reasonable: call loans on stock exchange collateral are, for instance, legitimatized at any interest rate agreed upon. There is another exception: a business corporation may not use usury as a defense when sued upon a loan. No purpose of this exception is explicit in the statute. One can surmise if one will that business men doing a going business for profit were regarded as the best judges of whether they could profit by borrowing at any rate offered. One can surmise if one will that the presence even in business dealings of the occasional squeeze in a temporary emergency was either overlooked by the legislature or was felt to be a hazard of business life which was no concern of the public's. The letter of the statute gives no light on this. Now certain lenders, in this state of the rules, have introduced a way of lending on real estate which displays ingenuity. A prospective borrower applies for a loan. He is told that the lender does not lend

13. [It is very important, however, to identify the source of doubt. If doubt exists only when language is unclear, as H.L.A. Hart seemed to suppose in *his* discussion of core and penumbral applications of a rule, then law may indeed for most applications (*not* the same as most judicial decisions) be relatively determinate. But if instead doubt exists when even clear language appears to dictate an unfortunate result—think of *Riggs v Palmer*, 22 NE 188 (1889) (the case of the murdering heir)—then the range of legal doubt expands exponentially, and the indeterminacy of law, as an empirical matter, expands with it.]

to individuals; that is not his practice, it is not his business. He deals only with corporate borrowers. If the borrower were to incorporate the real estate intended as security, that might become interesting. The borrower does. The loan is made to the corporation—a loan of $2700 against a mortgage at six per cent for the $4300.[14] When the borrower fails to pay, and foreclosure occurs, and the "individual borrower" seeks to attack the transaction as void, the point is ready that "the borrower" was by clear understanding the corporation, which by the clear rule of the statute can not be heard to argue usury as a defense. Now reasoning from purpose is as well established and as explicitly authoritative in the field of usury as in any portion of our world of legal rules, and all courts are agreed that however innocent and letter-perfect the "form" of the transaction, if the intent be to "evade the usury law," the court will "disregard the form and cut to the substance." To reason here from purpose and principle would lay close that when the only reason for incorporation is to procure the loan, and incorporation is suggested by the lender and made a pre-condition of the lending, then "the substance" is the adoption of the corporate form to "disguise" a loan made in essence to the individual, contrary to the purpose of the general usury rule. But to reason here from rule of thumb is to urge that the lender refused utterly to deal with any individual, lest he transgress the general usury rule by taking the bonus which he felt it necessary to get; and that the transaction was carefully channelled through another channel for the very purpose of meeting the explicit requirements of the explicit rule of exception, about business corporations. My judgment from a careful study of the situation, as of 1930, the time the matter was first presented to New York's highest court, is that the strong balance of probability and the fair guidance to be derived from the decisions, was that such a transaction as I have described it was "an evasion" and to be held void as against the borrower, seen as in truth an individual; and that lenders who wished to use this device would have been well-advised either to make their bonus charges low enough to seem extremely reasonable, or else to make them high enough to cover a terrific gambling risk.[15] But such a case, lost by the lender at trial, and lost again in the appellate division, had when it reached the Court of Appeals been put in the hands of a superb advocate. He won.[16] Against advocacy of

14. [Presumably Llewellyn intended "more than six percent," for the whole point of the example is that the transaction would be void under the "more than six per cent" usury law were it made to an individual.]

15. [Llewellyn's assessment of the law as it existed prior to 1930 appears to be based on *Union Dime Savings Institution v Wilmot,* 94 NY 221 (1983).]

16. [Presumably Llewellyn is referring to *Jenkins v Moyse,* 172 NY 521 (NY 1930).]

equal caliber it is difficult to see how he could have won. One uncertainty is here demonstrated: the trial court and the Appellate Division were quite clear that the rules told them to class the transaction as a covert loan to the individual; the Court of Appeals told them there was no evidence to maintain that classification. But another uncertainty results as well: for the Court of Appeals took not only the less appealing line of technique, it took a line of technique which in a future usury problem, with no such superb advocacy present on the lender's side, *it cannot be relied upon to take again*. Indeed, in any distinguishable aspect of the general usury situation, the same advocate, appearing this time for the borrower, could almost be guaranteed to win, even against an opponent of his own metal.[17] This is the *double* type of uncertainty of the meaning of the rules which advocates' leeway, left unstudied and uncontrolled, produces. First, insufficient imbalance toward the less probable and less reasonable outcome can unpredictably produce that outcome.[18] Second, where it does, the precedent thus made is less certain of implication, less solid to work with and build on, than it would be if it had been "right." Above all, such a precedent interferes with one of the most solid lines of lawyer's work we have: the diagnosis of the *attitude or temper* of a court in a given field of law, which, when it is stable, does guide the bar in reading the rules of law.

The reasons why advocates' leeway lies unstudied, why it remains *hidden* leeway, lie psychologically and sociologically very deep, and I shall not undertake to explore them. I shall content myself with some of the more obvious factors. One of them, certainly, is that men are not comfortable with the feeling that there can be more than one "right" answer. Any of us can remember, if he will try, the emotional dissatisfaction he experienced when he first met square roots, and found that plus *or* minus two could be, nay, was, *the* answer. And I should not be surprised to find that when solution of a problem has been hard, the mind finds relief after solution is reached in closing itself against too sharp a memory of alternative possibilities, so that a judge who has turned to one line of our given techniques rather than another does not want, at that moment, to remind himself of how easily and

17. [Even if Llewellyn is correct that the outcome cannot be predicted on the basis of the existing formal legal doctrine, it is interesting that he concludes that the relevant variable is the quality of the advocacy, although it is possible that among the other possible explanatory variables are the individual characteristics of the lender, the individual characteristics of the borrower, the respect (or lack thereof) that the Court of Appeals had for the trial judge who first decided the case, the relationship between the statutory usury rate and the then-existing market rates, and many others.]

18. [There is a marginal question mark here, presumably Patterson's, but the sentence makes sense if we understand "toward" as "on the side of."]

legitimately he might have done the opposite.[19] In any event, if the answer sought is "the" right answer, and the answer arrived at is "the" right answer, in terms of emotion and conscience and duty, then a mode of discourse develops in which the advocate on either side puts his line of dealing with the rules and concepts as *the* right way. And he does not put it forward analytically as, among alternative possible ways, the right way for this case or this rule. He puts it forward in result, the rule seen along his chosen line, the case seen along his chosen line, the outcome dictated along his chosen line, and the outcome given all the flavor of desirability the advocate can muster. The choice before the tribunal, in such a discourse, appears to be one between rules, or between alleged "right" meanings of a rule, or between alleged "right" classifications of a state of fact, or between desirabilities, broad and narrow, of rival outcomes. I hope I am not simply ducking a difficult job of analysis and phrasing if I suggest that in regard to our *methods* of using our techniques for reading and working with rules and concepts we in our legal system are less sophisticated, are less carefully conscious, are more legally primitive, than in, for instance, we are in the framing of our private documents, where we try to make words neatly cover the wanted ground. For it seems to me that our opposing rationales of the opposing techniques live among our lawfolk side by side like cliff-dwelling city neighbors who pass each other without interest in each other. It seems to me that they live beside each other as the wisdoms and guidances caught into proverbs live beside each other among our lay folk. "Still water runs deep"; "Still water runs stagnant." "[N]othing ventured, nothing gained," and "Faint heart ne'er won fair lady"; but "A rolling stone gathers no moss," and "It's dogged as does it."[20] Such proverbs are not limited to lay affairs. The rules of law of the Bantu of Africa are, most of them, in proverb shape, and so were a great body of the medieval German rules; and such writers as [Robert Sutherland] Rattray, [?] Spieth, or even [?] Gutmann, are persuasive that proverbs can give a deal of guidance on the legal side. Yet in regard to the rules of law we feel, and feel with justice, that our legal system has taken a material step in undertaking to explore the areas of overlapping, and to catch into

19. [Llewellyn's 1930s intuitions turn out to be supported by considerable more recent psychological studies on cognitive consistency and the desire to reduce cognitive dissonance. See, for example, M.R. Lepper, M.P. Zanna, and R.P. Abelson, *Cognitive Irreversability in a Dissonance-Reduction Situation,* 16 J Personality & Social Psychology 191 (1970).]

20. [As the ensuing sentences make even clearer, these paired but opposing proverbs plainly provided the impetus for Llewellyn's famous later observation that much the same situation existed with respect to the canons of statutory construction. Karl N. Llewellyn, *Remarks on the Theory of Appellate Decision, and the Rules or Canons about How Statutes Are To Be Construed,* 3 Vand L Rev 395 (1950).]

communicable form guidance as to *when* the one competing wisdom calls for application, *when* the other. It is my suggestion that what we have thus done, in general, in regard to marking the rough area of application of one rule of law off from that of its neighbor or competitor is what we have not done, and need to do more systematically about our *techniques* and the rationales of our techniques for using, reading, "applying" our rules of law and concepts. "A statute in derogation of the common law is to be strictly construed" and "A remedial statute is to be liberally construed so as to effectuate its purpose" look to me strangely like two propositions of diverse implied counsel about "Still water." A scheme for guidance in construction of statutes would seem to call also for communicable indication of how to tell a statute in derogation from a remedial statute. If this be left intentionally to intuition, or judgment unguided, I suggest that intention could do with revision, in a complex world. If it be left unintentionally, because the problem has not been thought about, I suggest that the word "primitive" is an apt description of the level of juridical method.

Let me recall that "primitive" is not in this book a term of reproach. It is a term of description. It refers to that level of lumping or fusing ideas, or of trust in institutions just to work out somehow, which precedes the taking of conscious thought about analysis of the matter and the undertaking of purposeful regulation. Primitivity in this sense is an asset to a legal system *wherever it works well*—an asset because primitivity does its work with vastly less labor-strain than do more sophisticated techniques; an asset also because attempted analysis so easily goes wrong, and purposeful regulation so easily runs itself into unsuspected snags. But where primitivity does not work well, it needs attention. And in this matter of leaving the nature and effect of advocates' leeway hidden, I suggest that it disserves our legal system and that system's purposes as greatly as, say, in the matter of well labeled situational concepts it has served us. And the nature of primitivity in institutions is not unlike the nature of advocacy: if it is working well, you do not notice it; it is the creaking or bumping of the machinery or of the result which gives the signal for taking conscious thought.

Indeed we have here one further and major factor both in the hiddenness of the advocate's leeway and in its extent: advocacy achieves perfection when it makes itself appear unnecessary. Tribunals consist of men, and men prefer seeing of themselves to being guided or urged into seeing. Tribunals consist of judges seeking the right solution, and no solution is so right as that which is obvious. To perceive the "obvious" is to forget who made it "obvious." Among the lawfolk runs the proverb about the hero of the hour: "Have you ever heard Davis state a case? Man, when John W. Davis has finished the statement of the facts, there is nothing left to argue!"[21] Taken out of the context of fellow-craftsman's tribute, and put into the context of what this means to certainty of legal rules, this is itself a case which will stand restatement, twice. First: "When *John W. Davis* has finished the statement of the facts, there is nothing left to argue." Second: "When John W. Davis has finished the 'statement' of 'the' 'facts,' there is nothing left to argue." To paraphrase into the terms I have been using, he so presents the problematical situation, he so arranges its order and language of presentation, and its color, that as the situation becomes clear to be seen by all, it becomes clear also *by direct primitive perception* as raising the particular line of legal problem which Mr. David wants it to raise, and no other and more embarrassing line; the situation may even, as it becomes clear to be seen by all, already by direct primitive perception be clear also as fitting under whatever concept of our given legal system is part of a rule of law that dictates judgment for Mr. Davis' client. "It is always a pleasure," a distinguished and shrewd judge can then say, as you talk the case over with him, "to hear Mr. Davis argue; but I do not wholly see why you are so eloquent in praise about this particular argument. I had thought the case reasonably clear." It was indeed. *After* Mr. Davis or the advocate of similar caliber had finished "stating" it. And here I beg leave to note that the judge who knows himself alive to the advocate's leeway and the advocate's arts, and proves that by anecdote and instance, will still be found making his point on cases where the advocacy he is discussing *failed* to carry him along. Even such a judge will tell you rarely indeed of how the advocate whom he agreed with so shaped the case up as to make him see it that way. Which seems to me instructive.

But the hiddenness of advocate's leeway is not confined to judges; it extends to the advocates themselves. Indeed, were this not so, it is hard to see how the advocate who mounts the bench could suddenly forget so much of what he knew while still an advocate. The fact seems to be that it is a rare advocate who himself has a clear notion of how wide the leeway, which he uses, is; and none too common an occasion when an advocate who is stretching the leeway feels that the stretching is not that type of healthy correction which it is the business of the advocate to further, and of the court to accomplish. For our system of advocacy, here again, is more largely of the primitive than of the sophisticated, though it has its mixture of the

21. [John W. Davis, solicitor general of the United States from 1913 to 1918, losing (to Calvin Coolidge) candidate for President in 1924, founder of the Davis, Polk law firm, and losing counsel in *Brown v. Board of Education* (347 US 483 (1954)), was widely regarded as the premier appellate advocate of the first half of the twentieth century.]

two. The primitive legal approach, keeping law-stuff in undifferentiated fusion with law-stuff, calls for a lawyer to serve justice, to so move as a technician that "right" for his client results. By the same approach, it is the advocate's proper part to believe in his cause. And, as usual, there is health in primitivity. And, as usual, the very layman who knows, on a level more sophisticated, that the technical order is not the general social order, that "law" may not always be simple justice and may not in a given case serve even long-range justice, and that the going legal system gives a client claim not merely to "right," but to his "legal rights"—that very lawman is partly caught in the ideology of his lay brethren, and feels his touch of discomfort when he does not like the cause which he contends for. Sometimes pure pride and pleasure in technique can keep down such discomfort; and some men, hard-eyed, grow calloused in the matter. Most keep this piece of primitivity alive. And, again, most meet its emotional urge by acquiring belief in their successive causes. An advocate's views and beliefs take color from his client. Cast as a spokesman, he becomes a principal. The layman mocks at the lawyer's easy conscience; the mocker overlooks that there are two sides to most controversies, and rarely all the decency on either; he overlooks that fighting is a game which builds up loyalty and belief and righteousness of heart; he overlooks the emotional need of a normal man—even an advocate—to be *whole* in his work. These matters lead advocates to see each successive cause as right to win. The other lay factor, that right seems somehow single; and that pervasive factor, that the right and true and "obvious", when discovered, relieve and gladden and wipe out the memory of the countervailing possibilities; these also play in. The advocate receives his case, turns it in his mind, shapes it and rearranges it against this and that view of the rules of the law. It looks better and better, as he turns it. The rules of law—with all their own leeways in flux and fusion—shape themselves around the case. A "theory of the case" puts out buds, and blossoms suddenly. From then on, the matter moves in terms of rules of law, of decisions, of concepts, seen only in terms of what support they offer, or of how their seeming obstacles can be removed. And the *argument* shapes itself into *deductive* form, from premises which the tribunal is to take as already there and compelling, through "obvious" application to the case, on into the conclusion which is not only "right", but necessary. So far as the techniques of advocacy now become conscious, they become ways of making the court *see* what the advocate has come to see. Opposing counsel is just one more obstruction. Where is room left to meditate on how much leeway the advocate has discovered and exploited in the period—the unpleasant period—of puzzlement and flux, *before the light broke*?

There are cynical lawyers, of whom no such picture holds; but they do not affect the climate of opinion about advocates' leeway. For the most part, they do not talk; effective action, not the revealing of trade secrets, is their stock in trade. If they do talk, they shock. The shocking is not listened to. But for most advocates, most of the time, the matter lies as I describe it; they are irked even to listen to a recital of a state of fact until they find out which side to be on; pleasure in technique carries them through occasional cases where there is too patently no rightness in the cause; for the rest, they see what the right is in their client's case, and when they have found a way to make the court also see it, that is that. Let me add one more thing; an advocate who has lost a case is very commonly persuaded either that the court went wrong, or troubled in his mind about how he came to miss the right way of winning it. Before it is decided, he knows, also, that the outcome may be uncertain; and so—if he should carry that perception through—that there is uncertainty about the positive meaning of the relevant rules. But he has framed his case upon what he puts forward as certain rules of law. He will frame tomorrow's case upon what he puts forward as upon *certain* rules of law. He has no other basis upon which to frame any case than upon something to be put forward as *certain* rules of law. The general assumptions and general ideology of his art and profession, those general assumptions which are the only basis on which he can work, drown out cumulative meditation upon what the series of endless single uncertainties must mean, if put together. And so he does not know *of* the leeway whose existence is the main reason and the main support of his.

The reasons why the *net* impact of advocate's leeway seems peculiarly great in our system rest on the multiplication into the range of leeway and its hiddenness of three other factors. First, there is our reliance upon the case-to-case course or happenstance of adjudication for the development of our rules;[22] which means that advocate's leeway plays directly into their authoritative making and remaking, not merely into phases of "application" which would be easy to discard as mistaken. This, although English rules of law are taking on a much more settled structure than ours, both in range and clarity of statutory rules and in greater precision of case-law rules, this we share to some extent with modern England. But modern England has a single highest court for all its rules, and we have not; and there comes thereby to us a materially greater range of choice, range of phrasing, range of room for advocates to work in. That is the second factor. I do not know

22. [On this problem, see Frederick Schauer, *Do Cases Make Bad Law?* 73 U Chi L Rev 883 (2006).]

whether to add to it a further aspect, and urge that fact-situations change and complexify rapidly with us, and that the more novel or the more complex the situation, the greater is the room for its effective shaping in presentation by the advocate. And I must remind that while the skilful advocate can and repeatedly show [his] to be simply and inevitably *the* right answer, the same answer we should beforehand have taken to be the right answer[23]—that fact does not remove our factor of *anticipatory* uncertainty even when he does. For we did not know beforehand that he would not be on the other side, nor what he might accomplish if he were. No matter how skilful, even he may fail to win. It is the unpredictability of what *will* happen, within the leeway, which is the trouble.

The third factor goes to our personnel. I doubt whether any developed legal system has ever offered quite the variety among its lawmen that our[s] does—variety in training, variety in personal background, variety in skill, variety in insight. So far as the judges vary, there is an extra differential range for advocates to move in. A judge strong-minded, clear-headed, skilled and intuitive can cut advocate's leeway to that minimum which disturbs certainty not at all because it merely parcels out the labor of [the] effective study of the facts and the background of the rules at work, marshalling the results and urging the rival values that call for consideration. A judge lacking any of these qualities opens pro tanto the field for the advocate to shape results. If we do not know in advance which kind of judge will get the case—or will get the case first, and start the ball rolling—then we meet uncertainty due to range of official personnel. If we do not know what variant of case will turn up first, and our judges are sensitive to the flavor of the particular case, and our advocates quick to use that sensitivity—then we meet uncertainty due to our case-to-case method of building law as cases happen (or are made to happen) to arise. But there is a final matter in which the discrepancy of personnel hits with peculiar force. We have no match-maker who pits heavy-weight advocates against heavy-weights, and sees to it that champions have set against them not hams, but at least contenders for the championship[.] [So] in skill our lawyers range from champion to tyro, and in weight from unlimited to less than fly. This gives us often a *net* leeway of the advocates in our cases which is a bit awful to contemplate.[24] This, partly, on the side of justice and the client. And partly on the side of guidance and

23. [Here Llewellyn describes in terms of advocacy something very close to what Ronald Dworkin has described is the inherent nature of legal decision making. Ronald Dworkin, *Taking Rights Seriously* (Harvard 1978).]

24. [Although less awful if advocacy skill is less causal of outcome than Llewellyn, especially in this Chapter, supposes.]

control by rules of law. For as I have said before, it takes skill, intuition, and time to harmonize clear guidance by rules with rough justice in the end-result of adjudication. Lacking good advocacy, the "right" side represents the court either with nothing to be clearly seen, felt and responded to, or else the whole burden of inventing a technical solution under pressure of time and work, or else with the conscience-burden of just bulling through. If the court does not muster of its own initiative the wherewithal to meet the middle burden, then we have both [a] bad outcome and bad rules for future, and none too certain[,] guidance; or else we have [a] good single outcome, but accompanied by muddle of and for rules. Earlier, in the matter of the usury case, I attempted to show how skilful use of advocate's leeway can becloud the rules. Here let me set the counter-point: the beclouding by unskillful use of that leeway. There are of course berries on the bramble: when skilful advocacy and sanity for our legal system in the client's cause go hand in hand, then in no legal system of the world can a non-official so sweetly shape the spinning clay of law upon the wheel.

But if our rules of law have as their office to *clearly* guide, and even to control, both us and our officials, then the spasmodic impact of our advocate's leeway is too great for comfort. There are, fortunately, ways of reducing it. They are ways, fortunately, which can be put into practice at any moment by any court which wishes to. They require, for introduction, no change by statute, nor any change in the rules of the game, nor any acquiescence by an ultimate court, nor any regeneration of the scheme of things. Amusingly enough, any judge who would pick up for use these ways of reducing advocate's leeway would find his own work measurably eased and furthered by their use.

For they consist in nothing but an ordered and systematic use of the type of inquiry from the bench which in unorganized and spasmodic form has from the beginning been a part of our tradition. Are the technical rule of law and concept under discussion to be treated rightly as a thumbish matter? In more conventional phrasing: What is there to show that the technical rule and concept under discussion are of the type in which administrative convenience, fixed phrasing, sharp and rigid delimitation, and the use of unambiguous external criteria are of major importance? If it be shown that not rules and concepts in general, but this rule and concept in relation to such cases as that in hand, are properly regarded as of this character, and if it be shown satisfactorily why that is so, then further discussion of purpose, justice, and the peculiar ethical merit of the case in hand has little meaning. If, on the other hand, that be not shown, then argument is properly directed to and held upon the reason underlying the rule and concept, upon the purpose of the statute, and upon what reason there is for thinking an alleged reason or purpose to be *the* reason or purpose—and the case in hand takes on meaning in the light of that. We have the two methods of handling our authoritative materials. We have, even in their extremes, the two types of authoritative materials to be handled. We have the court's privilege and practice of indicating what it is which the court peculiarly desires to see cleared up. There is no doubt in my mind that any appellate court, would, on review, note with interest a suggestion in an opinion from below that the rule concerned was one whose purposes were, for a reason duly given in terms, furthered by rigid phrasing and by fixed application, attending to external marks. Th[ere] is no doubt in my mind that an appellate court would note with equal interest a suggestion in an opinion up for review that, for a reason duly given in terms, the rule concerned was one of those whose underlying reason was of the essence, and that that reason, duly set forth in terms, called for a given disposition of the case. I am urging that such an attack on the problem of a case in any opinion by a lower court would neither shock nor disturb nor arouse distaste or distrust, but would on the contrary somewhat quicken interest, and would somewhat sharpen the appeal of the relevant (and of course wholly familiar) line of technique.

And let me not be mistaken. The juice of what is being suggested lies in the *reasons* being "duly given in terms." I do not want the word "principle" which I have used to describe one method of work to be confused with the looser uses of that term among our lawmen. For "principle" is used, as a word, in our law-writing and law-thinking to include ways of word [use] and frequent [use of] specific propositions which are in at least one half of their nature rule-of-thumbish. The term which to our lawmen unambiguously indicates what I am speaking of as work on lines of "principle" is work along the lines of the *reason of the rule*, or concept. For in looser moments laymen say "on principle" when they mean "For reasons I shall not bother to recite, and certainly not to think about further, and perhaps have not thought about at all." And, in their moments almost as loose, they can set forth as "The principle which controls the situation" or "The true principle involved" a formulation whose only resemblance to what I am talking of lies in its being a line of escape from particular words or particular precedents. Indeed one can fairly say that one power attributed to any formulation when a layman dubs it a "true principle" is that it is to serve, and can claim to serve, as a basis for judgment not only independently of any countervailing authoritative and more explicit words, *but also independently of any examination of its own underlying reason*. This should not be so, and in the stricter and sounder usage of our lawmen it is not so, but the flavor and smell of the word "principle" is the flavor and smell it has acquired in the hands of those who have fled to it to save themselves from clear thought and clean analysis, from the labor of cleanly articulating for technical use rules which combine appealing end-results with clarity and the authorities. It is not therefore any talk in an opinion about "principle" which I see as a sound approach to appeal to any appellate court. The *talk* in the opinion, like advocate's talk to a court, should run in terms of *the reason* of the rule or concept. For "the reason of" a rule or of a concept or of a statute has this unmistakable flavor among all our lawmen and in any context: it requires to be made *explicit* to be listened to. (Contrast "On principle.") And it requires to do what a "principle" purports not to require to do: it requires by its formulation and in its formulation to give reason for it to be taken as *the* reason, and to persuade that there *is* reason for it to be taken as *the* reason.

An illustration may be needed, of this. It is accepted on all hands that there is a "principle" that an offer which envisages acceptance by continuing action of the offeree—say building a dam—is revocable, without leaving any obligation on the offeror, up until the moment of completion of the "requested performance". Writers and judges who discuss the matter say that this is unjust, impractical, and a touch outrageous. Which is right. But it is "strict principle". Departure from it wins praise; hesitant praise, because it is a departure from principle; but praise, because the departure, properly limited, makes sense. In such a situation, "principle" means (1) widish generalization (2) correct and authoritative and compelling (3) and-of-course sufficient to overcome any variant "anomalous" more particular authority within its orbit. It does not mean: giving its *reason* on its face. It means: to be taken as correct *even* when the result shocks any reason but itself. In this sense, "principles" of law are guides through the rules of law, and rule of thumbish "principle" can guide through rule of thumbish rules. But in another sense our lawmen speak of the "principle of the rule" as they do of its reason; and other "principles" are guides to the search of justice, such as that "He who seeks equity must do equity," or that where exchanged performances are contemplated, each party must be ready to do his part before he can effectively call upon the other to do his. It is this latter usage which I am approximating here, when I speak of work along lines of "principle," and I should be sorry to be mistaken in the matter. It is not merely the line of escape from external marks which is in mind, nor merely the authority and correctness of the formulation, but, and especially, the appearance of its reason on its face: for that is what makes for guidance and even certainty in dealing with the uncharted detail. And the matter of width of generalization, as I have said before, is of no moment to my usage; a very narrow concept, say "deserted wife in need"[,] can be built singingly[25] along lines of "principle."

And let me in another point be not mistaken. I am not urging that any device for winnowing, for clarity's sake, the rule of thumb cases from the rule-on-lines-of-principle cases, would work magic. Nor am I urging that there is no uncertainty left when rule of thumb cases are approached by rule of thumb techniques, and rules and concepts built on principle are approached by the techniques appropriate to them. What I am urging is that a conscious effort to winnow, followed by a conscious effort to force joining of argument along the appropriate lines, would be a noble first advance upon a neglected field of high uncertainty in our rules of law, their meaning, and their work; and would even in itself contribute *in any individual case,* and if generally adopted would contribute then[,] in general, to materially *reducing* the size of that field of uncertainty, and *reducing* the quality and degree of the uncertainty within it. I am urging that the lines of approach suggested are simple enough, manageable enough, sufficiently rooted in the ways of our legal system, to give moderate guidance to the heterogeneous average among our personnel, and to give guidance along moderately similar lines. I am urging, finally, that the use of such lines would and would have to further also *control* of their own use, since the mere presentation, along such lines, of adjudications for review forces the type of review which furthers clarity. And I am inclined to urge another thing: that one sees here some evidence that the road to a sounder general dogmatics lies in study of why we have come to have the general dogmatics which we do have—all of it being looked at, at once, and each portion being taken as probably appropriate in its proper circumstance.

[Add the manufacturer development as technical App.][26]

25. [In this context meaning "overtly," and Llewellyn often talked of the "singing reason," the reason—or rationale, or justification—for a law that was spelled out or announced in the law itself.]

26. [This is Llewellyn's note to himself, but there is no indication that he ever actually added the material or wrote the Appendix.]

CHAPTER VIII

Stabilities within the Leeways

In our search for better understanding of the work and meaning of rules of law we have found ourselves, almost inevitably, swinging back and forth between factors of stability and manageable certainty, on the one hand, and, on the other, factors of erratic change, factors making toward non-guidance. And the reader will have noticed a tone of regret whenever erratic change was under discussion; regret, but insistence that the unwilling nose be held close to the most unpleasant fact. The reader will also have noticed an absence of any regret at change; indeed he may have noticed a quiet assumption that *stability and manageable certainty* include a very respectable quantity and quality of change, whereas *erratic* movement is *introduced* into a legal scheme of things by conscious effort which is directed toward keeping movement out of it.

At any rate, if these matters have not yet been noticed, let them be noticed now. *Stability* and *change* are, in the world of law, no proper contrast. Each word is a word of necessity, and each is a word of moderation and of wisdom. *Rigidity*, on the other hand, and *erratic change*—these are words of unwisdom and of non-necessity; they are a proper contrast, they are contrasting evils. *Stability in change* is the desired substitute for both. For stability in things of law is not the absence of change. Stability consists rather of sufficient order in change, sufficient primitive approach to imperceptibility in change, to make change non-disturbing, even anticipated as it occurs—to make any failure of the impending change be felt as a disturbance, as a pinching by the past, as a "technicality" in that invidious sense which means that it comes to notice only as a thing which ought already to have been ironed out. For when our law officials feel some ineptly phrased technical rule of law in terms less of its words than of some sound core within it, and then allow the pull of the relevant portion of the social order to induce remodelling of that rule's unsoundly indicated edges; or when, while working still with the core and in it, they give new, needed direction or impetus to that core—that is change, on the technical surface, and it may even be change in the underlying technical substance. Twenty years ago, for instance, a benefit scheme for employees who remained in service twenty years or until they died, certificates in which made it perfectly clear that no *legal* obligation was being assumed by the company—twenty years such a benefit scheme created no legal rights in an employee or his wife or sister. Today the chances are strong to the contrary. Twenty years ago and today two things were equally clear to see: the company's expressed non-desire for legal obligation, that is one; the expectation and reliance of the employee, that is the other. The balance tips, and the result differs, and the transaction shifts meaning, and the technical rules of law shift meaning also, according to how these two clear and conflicting elements get weighted by a court. A change in weighting is indeed a change. But it is a change which has nothing in it of the unstable. It is the proper doing of what has always been done by proper lawmen as officials, and of what in the sane view of a sane technician would be seen *in advance* as a constantly impending and inherent *part* of *any* technical rule of law which we may have. The ideal of such continuing readjustment is part of the meaning of the words of *any* rule,[1] and the machinery for working such readjustment out is part of the institution through which *any* rule gains all positive meaning that it has. The occurrence of remodelling or redirection is indeed a *maintenance* of stability because it decreases tension between the technical order of law-rules and the general social order in its relevant aspect. Decrease of such tension *never* strikes the relevant layman [as] a phenomenon of instability, nor does it strike the general uninterested or disinterested law "public" so. Nor does it so strike any lawman who is sensitive to law's purposes or to the effective ways of our legal institutions. It upsets one class of persons only. And it is a class which greatly needs upsetting. It upsets any lawman (and perhaps their ill-advised clients) who have allowed themselves[,] against the better instincts and practices of their trade and brethren, to build up expectations out of the words of rules *alone*.

1. [That this "continuing readjustment" is a feature of legal decision making in some legal systems is not necessarily the same thing as it being part of the "meaning" of the rule, and in treating the former as an inherent part of the latter Llewellyn implicitly aligns himself with, for example, Lon Fuller, and against those, including the editor, who would seek to distinguish the meaning of the rule from the question of what some legal decision maker should do with it. See Frederick Schauer, *A Critical Guide to Vehicles in the Park*, 83 NYU L Rev 1109 (2008).]

To see that the type of change we are in discussing is in truth change, one needs only to put into precise propositional shape what the rule was before the change and what, by the change, it has become. That shows up the alteration which inheres in "mere interpretation or application." But such change not only maintains "continuity with the past," it not only represents a "development of our received materials of decision;" it does much more; it is the only way of keeping us from breaking with many portions of the past, it is the only way of so developing particular received materials so that the product continues to be received. And I repeat that to any layman who does not happen to be interested in capitalizing (irrespective of the public weal) the accidental language of the older technical phrasing, such change in the words and even the direction of a rule of law comes not as a disturbance, but as a gratifying evidence that that much, at least, is right with the law and with the judges.

Let me say the thing over again this way: Any rule of law which has not been given frozen verbal form (as a statute has) can always be treated and stated on a level of broad abstraction or on a level of narrow near-concreteness.[2] And even the statute can be dealt with, in terms of its "purpose" or "principle," in similar fashion. Now *technical* exactitude of meaning, in *advising* any particular person or group just where they stand with reference to "the" rule of law, or in *deciding* where any such person or group stands—such technical exactitude can undergo any quantity of change, can go into exact reverse over most of the relevant field, and can yet be utterly hidden from confession of change by shoving the statement of "the rule" up into higher abstraction. As thus abstractly stated, "the rule" "remains unchanged" (like "the principles of the Constitution.") The technician wins or loses cases, or decides cases for plaintiff or defendant, and the litigant pins liberty or fortune, upon the more narrow and concrete phases [phrases?] of rules of law. The citizen who is unconcerned is, however, quite content with shifting up the level of abstraction—*so long as the results suit him.* All the *legal* or technical continuity he needs is afforded by the most abstract of abstract principle, *so long as the result suits him.* "The skin of the living thought," the word, or the rule clothed in words, must, to suit the layman, give to the thought, and the thought must give to the felt need of the social order. If some portion of that social order undergoes change, then so must the thought of the legal rule, and if the thought changes, its skin ought as of course to change.

2. [Note that this is a claim about how some rule in some verbal form should be *treated,* and not a rules-standards claim about how rules should be written.]

This is not the conscious philosophizing of the layman. He does not thus philosophize. He simply primitives his way into these results. And stability, to him, is the régime in which changes go pretty much unnoticed, in which they give no greater bother, *because they keep pace one with another*.

The heart of understanding of this matter lies in understanding of its double primitivity. To the layman the accent and interest lie in the result. That is the basic primitive factor: the people and their law. The layman cares nothing whether the needed readjustment be[,] by shifting on the second level of primitivity, within the technical legal order—whether it be by a shifting of technical words or of the technical color of words which lawmen themselves will not notice, or whether it be by the more sophisticated primitivity of some ingenious conscious fiction which only a lawman could accomplish and only a lawman could indeed perceive to be needed, or whether it be by over explicit readjustment of the technical rules of law theretofore current. The layman's quarrel even with this last (and to him strangish) procedure will arise almost exclusively when he objects to the result. The point is made with peculiar force when one looks back over the shift in the attitude of our Supreme Court in the spotlight of the years just past.[3] It is a rare layman indeed who can be got excited over *how* it was done, over, for instance, whether the "new majority" are laying down new rules or are reinterpreting old rules; it is a rare layman who has any real interest in the question [of] whether the court's decisions make or merely "apply" Constitutional law. Most laymen simply assume the latter. Then they proceed to approve *any* action of the Court which suits their notion of current need, and to disapprove *any* action of the Court which does not suit their notion thereof. I, at least, have yet to meet a layman who criticized the Court's *reasoning* in a case *whose result that layman liked*. How often, for that matter, dos one hear lawmen doing that?

Now such is the stuff of stability in matters of law. And the first and obvious lesson from that observation is that *stability* is *not* in *our* legal system produced by the rules of law. It has to do with the management of those rules, and with their remaking at need and need's call. In what has gone before there has been some discussion of factors in the handling and manage-

3. [Llewellyn was writing this in 1939 or 1940, and plainly referring to the Court-packing controversy of 1937 (see Barry Cushman, *Rethinking the New Deal Court: The Structure of a Constitutional Revolution* (Oxford 1998)) as well as the various other high-profile cases in which the Supreme Court first struck down (for example, *Schechter Poultry Corp. v United States*, 295 US 495 (1935); *Carter v Carter Coal Co*, 298 US 238 (1936)) and then began to uphold (for example, *NLRB v Jones & Laughlin Steel Corp.*, 301 US 1 (1937); *West Coast Hotel Co. v. Parrish*, 300 US 379 (1937)) an extensive range of New Deal laws.]

ment of our rules which make, some of them for stability, some for erratic change, some now for the other; and before going further I shall attempt some summing up of such factors in this context. They are important, each and all, and in their more systematic study lies much help and hope. But the present chapter I want to devote to the part played in stability and also in guidance by a most complex and baffling phenomenon, one which it is highly ill-advised to take for granted and which deserves instead the same type of sustained study lavished so joyously through the centuries on the rules of law. I refer to the Office of the Judge.

[——————————————————][4]

For the layman does not want stability in the sense of technical rigidity. The "skin of the living thought," the word, or the rule, must, to suit him, give to the life of the thought, and the thought must give to the felt need of the social order. If in some portion that need undergoes change, so must the thought; and if the thought changes, so must the skin. Stability, to the layman, means that such changes shall remain unnoticed or noted simply as rights *because they keep moderate* pace one with another.

In much the same way, "manageable certainty" is used here to mean that type and degree of certainty which can be effectively achieved by the men and the devices which we have. A counsellor, where he can, shapes his work to build on the bed rock portions of the rules, and shapes his transaction to stand four-square despite all contingency of court or flavor of the case; almost to stand despite the contingencies of later advocacy. This makes out "manageable certainty." A strong shrewd judge grasps the essence of the situation, smithies it into tough words, his work finds favor, brings relief, and wears into the future. And this makes out "manageable certainty." Thus, on the one hand, the situational concept and our lawmen's sense of the heart of words, their feel for the meaning of impinging fact-material, as much as any coincidence which is achieved in line and rate of change between a portion of the technical legal order and the relevant portions of the order of our Great Society—all such things bring stability in change, without much management. Whereas good counselling, good judging, the good fortune of having advocate-balance sometimes show and thrust toward the good

4. [The manuscript of Chapter VIII as left by Llewellyn was in two parts. The first, titled "Chapter VIII" and with the chapter title, ended here. The second, titled "Chapter VIII (2)" and with no chapter title, seems not to follow smoothly from where the first part left off. Most likely is that a transitional page or more remains missing from the beginning of the second part, although another possibility is that even more is missing from what Llewellyn intended to be a fresh start on the chapter.]

way to what is needed, the well-built rule or concept on some needed line of principle: all such less primitive and more intellectualized procedures further "manageable" certainty. As does, so long as it fits, the pedestrian but effective well-built rule of thumb.

On the other hand, errors in technique, such as attempting to rivet an edged verbal pattern upon a changing scene, threaten us with judicial distress, and so with judicial unpredictability and confusion, and so with absence of the very guidance sought. So also do slips in the adjustment of our institutions such as those which open, in a regime of sought guidance in advance, the almost ungodly range of advocate's leeway which is with us (though the excelling advocate causes judicial distress not in his case, but only, when he was on the wrong side, after it.) Our partial failure, thus far, to work out harmonization of our gearings between the legislature and the judiciary must likewise be figured into the debt column here. And, by no means least, must be figured the fact that our jurisprudence and our rules of conscious dogmatics are only beginning to emerge from the proverb stage, are only beginning to see and pose for conscious study the problem of how to choose among those available and competing lines of technique which, in a given situation, will conflict in result.

In all of this, however, our eyes have been too much directed at the rules of law. And where we have found those accepted rules open or multiguous, our eyes have been too much directed at the accepted institutional techniques for *technical* handling of those rules of law. We should, as observers, be sad reporters to the gentleman from Mars, if we confined our observation to these two matters which have worked their way, in words, into the authoritative—and the less authoritative—books. We should be sad reporters if we confined our observation to the matters which, in our legal system[,] have been already at least partly verbalized. For if there is one thing we have seen it is that the verbalizations are partial, defective, mutually inconsistent. Whereas we know that one way or another, the system does go on. When a system does go on, despite its inadequate verbalizations, when it goes on though its accepted language about *how* it goes on is patently faulty, and when the rules for guidance which are accepted in the system as *the* rules for guidance are patently insufficient in themselves to make it go on guiding—then the observer must surely scout around for practices or ideas, for *some other* lines of guidance which have not yet got pegged down in the accepted language. Put it this way: *he must go scouting for the things which do so service and guide the system in fact that its work remains usable despite* the ways in which its people *try* to work.

I for one am no follower of that strange doctrine sometimes adumbrated which seems to suggest that if our current rules of law and our intellectualized techniques for dealing with them are shown in any area or at large to be in themselves ineffective to *control* officials, and often even to *guide* them, then we find ourselves cast upon the arbitrary action of officials—judges or others—as on a desolate and despairing reef. For there were judges before even there were rules of law, and before even there were recognized techniques of precedent or of construction of statutes or of "correct" use of whatever the authoritative materials may have been. There were *judges* who understood their office; and there were, too, *folk*, who set a standard for those judges to live up to. Departure was shameful, and men reached to blot out the shame. "The sons of Samuel walked not in their father's ways, but took bribes, and perverted judgment." Nor is the lesson peculiar to a single tribe. [Samuel] Pepys, for instance, not as a judge, but as an administrative official, wrestles with the problem through the years. At first, with an income inadequate to his desires, he takes gifts for the awarding of a navy contract. He finds an interesting line of reconciliation of his duty with his interest. He expects a gift from the lucky man. He expects it to be appropriate. He is willing to hear in advance what it will be. But (1) he will not take money. (2) He scorns a colleague who is taking gifts *in advance* of the award. In later years, as a more responsible official *and* with an income adequate to his notions, he not only repudiates gifts, but sees the practice as demoralizing to the Service and takes measures against it. Pepys, in a word, as an *administrative* official *in advance* of his age, goes through in one life-time a line of development which on the *judicial* side is recorded in [Francis] Bacon, who had Pepys'ed and already been thought off-color for doing so, and again in the great [Lord Matthew] Hale, whose resolution was to be sure to keep even his *servants* from taking favors from a suitor. In our day a Manton[5] is a national scandal because he is extraordinary; his removal profits not only the public, but the standing of the bench; all men see clear, and are glad to see clear, one thing that the judge's *office* must not be.

5. [Martin T. Manton, then the senior judge of the United States District Court for the Southern District of New York, was tried, convicted, imprisoned, and removed from office for conspiracy to obstruct justice—in essence for bribery—in 1939. See *Manton v United States,* 107 F2d 834 (2d Cir 1939), *cert denied,* 309 US 664 (1940).]

What concerns me here is that the taking of bribe and favor is but the crassest and most rule-explicit aspect of a tradition of the *Office*. Even the practice, hardly formed into a statable rule, of self-disqualification for one or another kind of possible bias, is but a gross and obvious externalization of a favor as clean to feel, as deep to permeate, as it is elusive to phrase. To be a *judge* is to be something other than oneself. It is to charge oneself with office as with electricity. The stupid man remains a stupid judge. The prejudiced man takes prejudice with him to the bench. The easy conscience, the arbitrary temper, self-glorificatory love of basking in the public eye—these do not suffer blackout under the judicial robe. Let that be conceded. What I do state as fact is that save in extraordinary cases, save in cases so infrequent as to be *for the system* (not for the poor devils who individually suffer under it) negligible, the degree to which judicial office smooths out such errors in the man, the *degree* to which he develops all that is in him to be developed of The Judge, is an astonishing and uplifting thing, a thing to hearten any citizen. If you will measure our judges on the bench not against some idiot picture of a marble lady with a scale and blinded eyes who somehow functions also as a slot-machine, but will measure them instead by what the same men were before they Sat, and even by what they now are when they are not Sitting, you will see a firm tradition shaping its people to a degree and with a power which in older sociological writing used to be set up as the achievement only of the machinery of a caste, working in [a] slow-changing culture from childhood on. I shall attempt to clinch this point by an extreme case. There sits on one of our high courts a judge long noted, along with his convictions (of, if you prefer, his prejudices, for I take "prejudiced" to be convictions too firm to shake, but disapproved by the describer), for his arbitrariness and lack of interest in either discussion or amenities. Called on to preside in the absence of the chief, the judge developed a fairness and even kindliness in handling the courtroom, a dispassionate evenhandedness in furthering discussion in the conference room, which struck emotion from brethren who had grown into a habit of finding him a colleague singularly difficult. That a double injection of the Office ideal could thus remake the whole behavior even of one on whom a first injection had seemed inadequate forces the suggestion that less stubborn material must yield far to the first impact.

But the fact is in the nature of a miracle. Consider that the judge has been, has been long, a lawyer; that he has been trained through the years by the very practice of his trade to see cases from a single side alone. Consider that there is among us no apprenticeship for the bench, nor even any book to teach a neophyte the strange and uneasy art of judging. Consider that such crucial matters as how to find right balance between justice and the technical legal order are almost nowhere made explicit even as problems, let alone as subjects of wise lines of guidance. Consider that the toughest judicial job, that of sizing up the fact-material *not* so as to make a case for one side, but so as to *focus the issue* around which the problem ought, for the common weal, to turn, is not discussed in any book, nor is it taught by any teacher. Consider that even "impartiality" is an ideal whose nicer phrasing baffles a philosophy. And *still* our concept and ideal of Judge's Office lays its hand upon men—for *healing*, for making them more *whole*.

What an Office and the ideal and practice of an Office may be, which can record such institutional effectiveness, deserves more study than is its common portion. It deserves study peculiarly when our explicit rules of law are under consideration to determine their effectiveness. This is not only because the work of the rules is seen more clearly when the screen of the Office is examined, through which the rules must pass to do their work in court, and to make vocal their more exact meaning for guidance of officials and laymen who hope to keep out of court. It is also, as has been suggested, because the true work of the rules of law, their very partial and spotty realization of the ideals which we a bit naively set for them, is hard to *face*, unless we can find some assurance outside the rules themselves that something of regularity, of evenhandedness, of sustained labor toward what our rules are for, is with us quite apart from the rules, and would still be with us, though the rules should prove more reed than oak to lean on. So that while I cannot hope to catch into words the whole or the living essence of what makes up the Judge's Office as it has developed through the centuries of our culture, it seems vital to attempt to make more explicit some phases of it, phases which tell, each one, against that "arbitrary disposition" of matters which looms overeasily as a bogey-man. The aim is not to exhaust nor even to describe, but rather to find some simpler illustrations of the *kind* of drive the concept of the Judge's Office carries.

One idea which is moderately articulate is that the judge is not to decide this case in any way in which he is not willing to decide a similar case with utterly different parties. I call this "moderately" articulate because what I am saying is *not* that it is his duty to decide the case under *a* rule of law, nor under a rule of law for all like cases. That is an idea quite articulate; it is articulate and standard doctrine. And it is serviceable doctrine. But underlying such doctrine are purposes which are only partly articulate in the doctrine itself; and one of those purposes goes to the concept of the Judge's office. "The judge is not to decide this case *in any way* in which he is not *willing* to decide a similar case with utterly different parties." "Way" is a word to search the judge's conscience. "Way" goes not only to finding an acceptable "ground" for decision. "Way" goes to holding down any conscious manipulation of the rule's leeways so as to bring out a personally or politically or otherwise satisfactory result because the judge wants to, for reasons which he can see or feel that *as a judge* he has no business to want to. "The judge is a friend of mine;" the fact that the case is of interest to the party; the fact that letters have been received which threaten "unless;" the desire about this case of a leader whose support can mean a longed-for nomination; the fact that the defendant belongs to some group or class distasteful to the judge or is personally unappealing—such are matters which the judge is, so far as in him lies, to put out of the case and his consideration of it. Some writers, aware of instances in which judges have acted counter to this phase of their tradition, and have skillfully covered their tracks (with or without help from skilful counsel)—some writers have on occasion been tempted to make game of the requirement that decision shall be "under a rule of law."[6] There is always, the argument can run, "a rule of law" to be had, for the case, or a twisting of "the facts" to make one unnecessary. Such writers are saying, and they are saying soundly, that *external control by external means* against such manipulation, our rules of law do rarely indeed, of themselves, afford us. But such writers if they stop with this miss the difference between *guidance* and *control*. And they miss also the difference between *compulsion* to phase *a* rule for the case, and guidance as to what ways *of going about that job* are proper ways. But there are not too many *judges* who miss this latter difference. And one of our greatest guarantees against this "arbitrariness" specter is that the strain and drive of the Judge's Office is to bring out so much of the man beneath the robe as scorns to fiddle with Justice; that the office elbows into the corner so much of the man as might like to play the case this way or that for non-Judge reasons, no matter how easily the play might be to cover, no matter how personally convenient the untraceable manipulation might prove to be. This goes a decent distance toward decreasing, among judges, the discrepancies which exist or did not exist among the same *persons*, seen as men. It does not eliminate those discrepancies. But how anybody who has even tried to figure why we have more than one judge on a supreme bench could ever have thought that any rules or any institutions could eliminate those discrepancies, is beyond me.

6. [Llewellyn may well be referring here to Jerome Frank, *Law and the Modern Mind* (Brentano's 1930), and to other Realists who stressed the role of personal characteristics of judges, lawyers, and litigants in explaining judicial decisions.]

Of institutions as they are we must expect what they can yield, and no more. What has been mentioned, which we may label the "urge to unselfing of judgment," gives no help against that prejudice which carries to its bearer conviction that it represents the social welfare. It is not "impartiality," because conviction of the welfare of the whole may lead to vigorous sympathy with one party as against the other and ought to. It is a quite distinguishable thing from that evenhandedness of the umpire on questions of disputed fact which gives each side its fair chance to present its case, and endeavors to keep *fact*-determination unclouded by sympathy or bias. It is the urge to keep out of play the interests of the individual beneath the robe. And, as noted, it cannot operate upon such parts of the individual as speak to *him* the language of potent welfare of society.

Neither does it give help against that advocacy which is so skilful as to make its advocated answer to the question in hand become "obvious and lucid." It thus leaves open much of advocate's leeway, and it leaves also open such variation in results as rests on judges' diverse perception-power or perception-manner in regard to direction and nature of one of their two major goals: that of justice (whether in its immediate aspect, to the parties, or in its broader ones, to the great society.)

But even in the variations thus present despite the urge to unselfing of judgment, there is another aspect of the Judge's Office which reduces the individual swing. It is vocalized in the slogan that it is for the courts to *apply*, for the legislature to *make*, the law. It is reinforced by the traditional (and sadly wasteful) theory that any judicial declaration or reshaping of rules requires to be retroactive. It throbs subtly under the judge's interest in right disposition of the particular case in hand and keeps live a suggestion from that very case that the next case may be quite as illuminating. It sums up the traffic signal: SLOW. The judge who "wishes to put the case on a broad principle," the judge who seizes on the occasion to examine and "illumine the whole field of controversy," is an extraordinary judge; genius or resounding flopper, he is extraordinary. A tradition of the office, which *controls* most of those in the office, and, most of the time, does not merely guide them, stands solid: a step at a time, please; a very small step at this very small time—no matter how strongly the judge may feel[ ] urge to move.[7]

7. [For the modern debates regarding so-called judicial minimalism, compare Cass R. Sunstein, *One Case at a Time: Judicial Minimalism on the Supreme Court* (Harvard 1999), with Frederick Schauer, *Abandoning the Guidance Function: Morse v. Frederick*, 2007 Sup Ct Rev 205.]

This tradition is reinforced by a different and independent factor: the pressure of review. The two factors coincide in line of pressure; but they are independent, as we can see by observing the work of benches not subject to review. They also go slow. Perhaps the bench subject to review goes slower still; I doubt it. My belief is that the closer pressure of the facts of the individual case upon the judge who sits at trials forces about enough extra give into the work of his "lower" court to roughly balance the pressure from the possibility of reversal. Much more difficult to estimate is whether the fear of possible reversal operates differentially upon judges of lower courts according[ly] as they consider the particular case before them likely or unlikely to be appealed. Speaking very broadly, and with consciousness of the range of phenomena involved—from the effects of the spotlight in a cause célèbre on through pigheaded stubborness in putting through a position once taken—speaking very broadly, I do not think the *bulk* effect of such difference to be important, though I do suspect the absolute number of instances in which such effects appear to be rather considerable. But the major effect of the possibility of review I believe to lie simply in general reinforcement of the general judicial tendency to stay on *safe* ground, if that be possible: to decide, if that be possible, within the clear *core* of meaning of the accepted rules, and within the clear *core* of justice. And so far as this belief may be sound, it represents a phase of the tradition of the Office which pushes all men in the Office into similar decision; which therefore not only guides importantly, but goes far toward control.

Now none of these phases of the tradition and the ideal, of the practice and of such vague concepts about the Office as we have—none of these seem to me to threaten arbitrary, unruly, willful action by the courts, simply because courts may come to see the leeways within which they move to have the rather liberal width those leeways have. And while I can conceive—with difficulty—of the tradition itself changing somewhat under that perception, yet there is one phase of it which I cannot conceive as changing, and that is the judge's sense of responsibility as a judge, in a legal system which has once developed the concept of that office which we do have, however vaguely we may have it. Indeed, I am unjust to our system when I speak of vagueness in the concept of the Judge in his Office, of "judicial" behavior. That concept is *intellectually* vague in the extreme; the efforts made to limn it in the Canons of Judicial Ethics of the American Bar Association, for instance, have something of the sure, deft draftsmanship of a three year old at work with a crayon on a wall. But unless I am much mistaken, there remains the emotional concept, the *picture*. And that picture of "judicial" behavior, though its lines be unverbalized, yet signals any departure from it as a departure, whether one can say exactly why, or not. That picture is in Carter's[8] words on custom "better than known—*felt.*" And in it what is known as arbitrariness has no place. Upon that picture plays the steady pressure of opinion, and of the internal opinion known as self-respect. Opinion is divided; and the pressure of opinion is diffuse; and opinion of peculiarly close, effective[,] and persuasive sort may work contra-judicially upon a judge. The point I would make is that the self-respect aspect of opinion selects with some automatic sureness which phase of divided external opinion its business is to select and reinforce.[9]

8. [James Coolidge Carter (1827–1905), lawyer and legal scholar, defender of the common law, and author of *Law—Its Origin, Growth, and Function* (Putnam's 1907).]

9. [This is where the handwritten manuscript of Chapter VIII ends, but there is no indication whether Llewellyn intended this as the end of the chapter.]

The Remaining Chapters

Chapter VIII.[1] *Normative Drives and the Struggle for "Law My Way."*

The technical normative drive: the strain of a body of rules, in the context, toward growing in one direction rather than another, and the resistance to any movement across lines of force.

The counsellor's normative drive: the organization of the stable and predictable elements; their exploitation and incorporation in working methods; the building of new instrumentalities in and out of them; the extra certainty where a counsellor can control any future advocacy.

Group normative drives: counsellors serve groups, and differentially. Who uses counsel. Who uses the best counsel. But groups generate norms apart from counsel. The nature of ways and expectations. Normation out of ones' own background into open areas or fields of conflict. The courts as followers in the open areas, selectors in the fields of conflict.

Interest pressures: distortion of "the" norm; aggressive claim; the premium on initiative and organization. Classes or "rucks" v. organized groups.

The play of all of this on existing rules, as distinct from new legislation.

Chapter IX. *Law's Function and Problem of Balance*

The ideal of the Whole. The fact of Going Whole. De facto balance in the legislature, and the Constitutional Court as a flywheel. The uninterested and the disinterested.

1. [Llewellyn labeled these thoughts about the three remaining chapters Chapters VIII, IX, and X, but presumably he intended this to be IX, X, and XI, since there were more or less eight already completed chapters.]

The institutional sublimate of the balance ideal in dealing with the rules. "Derogation" and "remedial" as reflections of groping for balance. "Relational thinking" as imposition of balance upon a situation. Printings v. writings as a modern problem for balance-thinking. Iron v. yielding rules. The need for a technique to hold down over-counselling.

"Purpose" and "reason" as balance-producing devices: how do you go about "finding" them? Again the lay-half v. the law-half of the judge.

"Justice" at large a social matter; "Justice" in the lesser not merely legislative, but for court and counsel.

The consequent range where we have no business to *control* judges by rules, but merely to guide them by good ones; and then to get good judges.

Chapter X. *Toward More Rational Rationalization*

Restatement briefly of the thesis that it is the working whole which needs rationalization.

Attempt at pulling out and putting down a dozen specific lines of attack, partly already presented, partly saved for the conclusion—such as the concept of the "implicit preamble" of a statute, as a device to make statutory interpretation more orderly and its techniques more explicit.

Or: Advocacy in drafting: making the protective clauses show their reason: good service to the client introducing a level of drafting which tends toward showing up the gouge.

Concluding reminder that everything in the book is obvious stuff familiar to the trade: the only problem is to get the obvious *arranged*.

INDEX